The Ultimate Guide to Successful BioPharmaceutical Sales Job Interviewing

M. L. Miller

Published by SoaringME Publishing

ISBN-13: 978-1-956874-18-1

CONTENTS

Preface

Dear Reader,

Welcome to *SoaringME The Ultimate Guide to Successful BioPharmaceutical Sales Job Interviewing*. As a seasoned recruiter, I have interviewed tens of thousands of candidates, and was responsible for over 150 pharmaceutical sales representative hires in my first six months as a recruiter back in 1997. During my first recruiting project, the Fortune 100 employer embedded me into the hiring panels and I was part of the debrief on the candidates after their interview. I went onto collaborate with a variety of both large and small employers, consistently delivering outstanding statistics that showed I was aligned to what the employers wanted.

After working on sales and sales management roles I moved onto non-sales executive-level biopharma recruiting. In addition to starting my own recruiting company, I founded SoaringME, that specializes in helping candidates improve their interviewing skills.

In this book, you will find all the information from my original book, The Ultimate Guide to Successful Job Interviewing, with additional content specifically tailored to excelling in biotech and pharmaceutical sales interviews. You'll learn everything you need to know to master the interviewing process and impress your potential employer. I will teach you what employers are looking for in biotech and pharmaceutical sales candidates, the questions for you to ask, and the red flags to watch out for during your job search. By focusing on demonstrating the value you can bring to the position, you'll maximize your chances of landing your dream job or promotion.

Whether you're starting out in biotech and pharmaceutical sales or looking to advance your career, this book will provide you with the insights and advice necessary to ace your interviews and advance your career.

Best of luck, and I'm confident that with this book's help, you'll ace your interviews and get the job or promotion that you're after!

M. L. Miller

Founder, SoaringME

If you enjoy this book, please give it a review.

Visit

SoaringME.com

for additional resources.

Introduction

As someone looking to pursue a career in biopharmaceutical sales, it's crucial to understand the interview process and what employers are looking for in a candidate. Whether you're interested in entry-level sales, senior/specialty sales, or frontline sales management roles, *SoaringME The Ultimate Guide to Successful Biopharmaceutical Sales Interviewing* provides insights and advice to help increase your chances of success in any job interview process.

Biopharma companies have developed rigorous hiring processes to find the best fit for their sales jobs and the organization, so it's important to prepare for the interview to maximize your success rate and reduce any anxiety.

Interview questions are designed to uncover information that the employer needs to decide who the best candidate is for the job. Your primary objective during the process is to demonstrate through your answers and actions that you are the best match to the ideal profile of who they want to hire.

This book teaches you what the interviewers are looking for and what the most successful candidates have done. Being dishonest in interviews is not the objective, but to demonstrate the value you will bring to the position.

Even candidates with a lot of career experience often fail in the interview process because it's unfamiliar. Confidence is key, and you can build your confidence by doing your research, organizing ahead of time, practicing answering interview questions, and understanding the interviewers' point of view.

In addition to answering interview questions, it's essential to ask employers questions and watch out for employer red flags. Not all biopharma companies have figured out their hiring process, but by following the advice in this book, you can increase your chances of success in any job interview process and ultimately receive a job offer in your dream biopharma sales career. Whether you're just starting out or looking to advance your career, this book will provide you with the insights and advice necessary to ace your interviews and advance your career.

This book includes all the general interview advice from my first book, *SoaringME The Ultimate Guide to Successful job Interviewing* that can be applied to any job, along with tailored advice specific to biopharma sales interviews. With this book as your guide, you'll be well-equipped to impress your interviewers and land your dream job in biopharma sales.

BioPharmaceutical Sales Career

A career in biopharma sales can be a challenging and rewarding path for individuals with a passion for science and building relationships with healthcare providers. Starting in an entry-level sales role is often the first step towards gaining experience and developing the necessary skills to succeed in this field.

Entry-level biopharma sales positions typically involve prospecting and building relationships with healthcare providers, with a focus on generating interest in the company's products. The ability to understand complex medical information and build relationships with healthcare providers is crucial to successfully close deals and generate revenue.

As individuals gain experience and prove themselves as top performers, they can move into more specialized sales roles such as senior or specialty sales representatives. These roles involve working with key opinion leaders, negotiating complex contracts, and developing strategic partnerships with healthcare organizations.

Frontline biopharma sales management roles require individuals to oversee a team of sales representatives and work closely with them to develop and execute sales strategies. This involves providing coaching and guidance to team members, analyzing data to identify opportunities for growth, and developing relationships with key customers.

From frontline sales management roles, individuals can continue to advance to executive sales management roles such as vice president of sales or chief revenue officer. These roles require strong leadership skills and the ability to adapt to changing market conditions. Other executive roles may focus on specific areas of sales, such as market access or medical affairs.

Throughout all levels of biopharma sales, a customer-focused approach is essential to building long-term relationships and driving revenue growth. Sales representatives must have a deep understanding of healthcare providers' needs and pain points and the ability to develop customized solutions that meet those needs. Technical expertise in the products or services being sold is also crucial, requiring a willingness to learn quickly and stay up-to-date on industry developments.

There are many different types of biopharma sales jobs available, including entry-level sales, senior/specialty sales, and frontline sales management roles. These roles can focus their selling in a variety of settings, including hospitals, clinics for a specific disease specialty, and long-term care facilities to name a few. By mastering the skills outlined in this book, you can increase your chances of success in any biopharma sales interview and ultimately receive a job offer in your dream career.

Understanding What Recruiters and Hiring Managers are Looking For

To succeed in any interview process, it is vital to have a comprehensive understanding of what the interviewers are seeking. The foundation of this success lies in spending ample time to grasp as much detail as possible about the ideal profile being sought.

When a company decides to create a new job, it's because they have a need in their organization, and if they find the right person, the company will be more successful. To identify the ideal candidate, companies start with outlining the duties required for the role and develop a profile of the best-suited employee. Depending on the organization's size, the hiring manager, Human Resources, Talent Acquisition, upper management, or a combination of these may create this profile. The profile can be influenced by the hiring manager's personal preferences, the team's current makeup, or the previous employee's qualities.

The ideal candidate's profile comprises hard skills, soft skills, and personality traits, and while these traits vary slightly from company to company, most employers seek some specific traits in a new employee. These traits might not even be mentioned in the job advertisement, but interviewers still evaluate candidates on them. In the chapter on *How to Stand Out from Others*, we cover how understanding these hidden traits can provide an edge over other candidates.

Here are the eleven most common universal traits that interviewers are seeking.

1. Effective communication skills.
2. Passion for that work.
3. Self-motivated.
4. Works well with others.
5. Competent.
6. Ability to take responsibility for work and mistakes.
7. Good problem-solving skills.
8. Honest.
9. Ability to listen.

10. Nice to work with.

11. Reliable.

To identify the perfect candidate for a job, companies typically have a list of desired qualities and attributes, including educational background, training, experience, and personality traits. These may consist of a college degree, specific major, certifications, industry experience, knowledge of relevant software programs or programming languages, and other tools required for the role. The ideal candidate's personality may be characterized by being coachable, drive for future advancement, good teamwork skills, or ability to work independently.

The interview process is a series of steps designed to assess how well a candidate matches this ideal person, with the goal of eliminating candidates who are not a good fit. The job advertisement, interview questions, and final decision on who to offer the job to are all based on this profile.

Understanding the profile for a job is critical to success, as every company has a preconceived notion of the person they want to hire. This profile can be divided into two sides: the skills or experience side and the personality or compatibility with the company culture side. By having a solid grasp of this profile, you can position yourself as the best-suited candidate and increase your chances of securing the job.

Here are the best steps to understanding the ideal profile for a specific job.

1.   Research 10-20 job ads for similar jobs. Make a list of the duties required and desired attributes listed in all these advertisements.

2.   Research the backgrounds of employees who are currently in similar roles. Look at the 10-20 LinkedIn profiles and the background they had before being hired for a job like the one you want.

3.   Ask contacts in your professional network what they think makes people successful in that job, or if they know what type of candidate that company prefers to hire for that type of role.

4.   Compile the attributes that repeatedly show up in your research. This is a great starting point for understanding what the interviewers are going to evaluate you against.

To succeed in an interview, it's crucial to understand the list of required and desired attributes listed in the job advertisement. These traits are usually listed in descending order of importance, and understanding them is crucial to your success. The *COMPANION WORKBOOK The Ultimate Guide to Successful Job Interviewing* includes exercises that can help you understand the job profile, which may include many unwritten desired traits that you'll need to research.

It's important to note that job profiles usually represent a wish list for the hiring manager, not an absolute minimum. If you match 60% or more of the job profile, you should apply for the job. Some managers may take a chance on a candidate who only possesses 60-70% of the desired skills if they fit the ideal personality and are trainable on the rest. However, it's unlikely that you'll receive job offers in most cases where you're only a 60-70% match, and you may not even be interviewed.

During the interview, make sure to highlight areas in your background that relate to the job profile and avoid providing irrelevant information. Your resume should show the overlap you have with the ideal profile, and you should provide more detailed answers during the interview. For example, a nurse or therapist job profile may include experience working with elderly patients, so you should highlight your experience in this area.

Understanding the ideal profile is essential, as demonstrated by a Vice President candidate I worked with who didn't advance after the first interview. Despite having the necessary education and skillset, the candidate displayed hesitation in making decisions and asking questions during the interview with the startup employer. The role called for an individual who could take charge, be assertive, and propel projects forward. This candidate's prior experience with large corporations, where they functioned as a mere cog in the wheel, was a better fit for their personality which did not align with the desired personality traits. It's crucial to note that comprehending the ideal profile does not imply pretending to be someone else, but rather showcasing how you meet the requirements through your conduct and responses during the interview process.

BioPharmaceutical Sales Candidate Profile

The biotech/pharma sales industry demands candidates with a diverse set of skills that are vital to the role. Effective communication is a cornerstone of success, as candidates must be persuasive in convincing healthcare professionals the benefits of prescribing their products. Additionally, the ability to build strong relationships and establish trust with stakeholders is critical. Candidates must also possess customer-focused skills, tailoring their sales approach to meet the needs of their clients. Continuous learning and adaptability are essential, given the constant evolution of the industry. Being able to make good decisions under pressure and resilience in dealing with frequent rejections are also crucial skills. Being outgoing and organized are also highly valued, as is having experience with specific therapeutic areas or call points.

During the interview process, companies evaluate candidates beyond their responses to interview questions. Open-ended questions that assess a candidate's communication skills and presentation style are valuable. Evaluating a candidate's experience with specific call points and settings, along with their ability to provide concise answers, can also help determine their suitability for the role. Additionally, the ability to ask closing questions at the end of an interview is a positive indicator.

For entry-level biotech/pharma sales jobs, companies usually require a bachelor's degree in a science or business-related field. Often companies want candidates to have prior successful business-to-business sales experience. Candidates must possess strong communication and interpersonal skills, be self-motivated and results-driven, and have a basic knowledge of the pharmaceutical industry and healthcare environment. They should be able to work independently or as part of a team, have a valid driver's license, and be willing to travel for work. Good organizational and time-management skills, basic computer skills, and proficiency with relevant sales software are also required.

For senior sales roles, companies seek candidates with 3+ years of successful biopharma sales experience, preferably in the same therapeutic specialty area and/or calling on similar settings. Experience in these roles is critical in building relationships and establishing trust with stakeholders. A proven track record of consistently achieving sales targets and the ability to adapt to new environments are also necessary.

Succeeding in the biotech/pharma sales industry demands a combination of skills and experience. Candidates must possess excellent communication, relationship-building, ability to learn technical information, customer-focused, continuous learning, adaptability, decision-making, resilience, outgoing, and organizational skills. Entry-level roles require a bachelor's degree and previous successful B2B sales experience, while senior roles demand industry experience with a preference for the same specific therapeutic areas or call points.

How You Will be Evaluated

Preparation is essential for a successful interview. Candidates who don't prepare are viewed as less professional and less interested, leading to fears of underperformance and short tenures if hired. The most successful candidates plan, understand the employer's ideal profile, organize their thoughts and memories, and relate their skills, experience, and traits to that profile.

Employers use the ideal profile to develop an interview process that evaluates candidates' suitability for the position. Interviewers may be experienced enough to ask individual questions, while others may use an interview packet. To understand what interviewers are seeking in your answers, imagine yourself as the interviewer looking for the ideal profile.

For example, imagine you're interviewing candidates for the Director or Senior Director of Regulatory Affairs role in a biotech company. Apply this same process to whatever job you're interviewing for to prepare for a successful interview.

Here is part of the job advertisement that explains the ideal profile that we're looking for:

Primary responsibilities include:

- Participates with key stakeholders to formulate regulatory strategies.
- Plan and manage integration of multidisciplinary regulatory programs into the project team development plans for all assigned projects.
- Lead the planning of and conduct meetings with regulatory agencies as appropriate. May represent the company at regulatory agency meetings as appropriate.
- Perform regulatory intelligence activities to keep current on the regulatory environment and competitive products.
- Provide the company with current and proposed regulatory and scientific issues.
- Manage and review safety reports and submissions.

Education and Skills Requirements:

- Demonstrated knowledge of the drug development process is essential.
- Knowledge of laws and regulations affecting the pharmaceutical industry and regulatory experience.
- Must have prior experience working with the FDA or EMA.
- Experience in successful NDA, BLA or MAA filings is essential.
- Prior management experience preferred. Must demonstrate the ability to work through others.
- Highly organized, with attention to detail.
- Advanced scientific degree preferred. B.A. or B.S. or higher degree(s) in the sciences, or health-related field minimum, with 7+ years of regulatory experience (Director) and 10+ years of regulatory experience (Sr. Director.) Demonstrates personal leadership and collaboration skills.
- Travel up to 25%.

To prepare for an interview, imagine yourself as one of the interviewers. I will provide you with an interview packet that contains a list of traits we are looking for in the ideal candidate and ten to twenty different questions for each trait. These questions are designed to assess the candidate's skills or experience and evaluate their proficiency in that area.

For instance, the packet for the Director or Senior Director of Regulatory Affairs role in a biotech company might include traits like regulatory strategy, leadership, communication skills, and attention to detail. Under each trait, the packet will provide questions that will help evaluate the candidate's abilities and how they fit the ideal profile.

By practicing this mental exercise, you can anticipate the type of questions that interviewers may ask and prepare accordingly. This way, you'll be better equipped to demonstrate how you match the ideal profile during the interview and improve your chances of success.

"Prior management experience preferred. Must demonstrate the ability to work through others." As you prepare to interview these candidates, here is how your packet questions might look for the management experience that we are looking for:

Management experience:

Q1: How do you give feedback to others, and how do you hold them accountable?

Q2: Tell me about a project that you led. What made it successful?

Q3: How do you manage stress among team members?

Q3: Tell me about a time that you influenced other team members on a project. How did that work out?

Q4: Describe to me a time when you managed somebody who was struggling.

Q5: How do you plan for your team members' professional development?

Q6: How do you handle conflict between team members?

Q7: Tell me about a time when you had to let a team member go. Why? How did they take it?

Q8: How do you motivate people?

Q9: How have you successfully delegated to others?

Q10: What is your biggest management weakness?

During the interview process, each interviewer will usually be assigned three to five traits to evaluate in the candidate. The interview packet contains a list of ten to twenty questions for each trait, and each interviewer will choose one question to ask the candidate. There may be some overlap where multiple interviewers evaluate the same skill, and the candidate's resume may affect the questions asked.

In addition to hard skills, interviewers are also evaluating personality fit and how long it will take the candidate to become a highly contributing member of the team. After all interviews are completed, interviewers will compare candidates in a feedback meeting and may develop a favorite candidate to advocate for. Candidates who create multiple advocates will have a higher chance of getting the job offer.

To succeed in the interview process, prepare well for each interview, regardless of the interviewer. Get into a relaxed, professional, and likable frame of mind to make a good impression. By doing so, you can create advocates and increase your chances of securing the job.

This is how your answers are analyzed.

As a candidate, every answer you give in an interview must meet the minimum credibility standard set by each interviewer. For example, taking credit for territory rankings or success in a sales position after just three months may not be credible if the typical sales cycle is six to nine months. Similarly, claiming to be downsized when your former company is hiring and expanding will also harm your credibility. Only credible answers will increase the strength of your candidacy.

Interviewers prioritize the strength of a candidate's answers when evaluating feedback and making hiring decisions. A strong answer leaves the interviewer with confidence that you could be a good employee, and the strength of your answer is directly related to the impression you leave with the interviewer. The hierarchy of impressiveness may vary depending on the type of interview questions and the industry or sector of the job.

Therefore, when preparing for an interview, pay special attention to how impressive your answers are likely to be. This will help you organize your thoughts and memories in a way that highlights your strengths and presents you as a strong candidate.

Hierarchy of impressiveness for interview answers.

1. Verifiable accomplishments. (i.e., awards, recognition, publications, or rankings.)
2. Accomplishments that are harder to verify.
3. Good success stories that directly relate to the job.
4. A good example of past success that indirectly relates to the job.
5. An example that demonstrates a personality trait that fits the profile.
6. Demonstrating personality traits during interviews.
7. Hypothetical answers describing what you would do in a future situation.
8. Showing related work experience. (Higher rank if successful during that experience.)
9. Opinion: self-descriptive statements trying to convince the interviewer how great you are.
10. Answering with a lot of words but avoiding the actual question that was asked.

11. Awkward silence.

12. Lying.

Although companies do not have a formal hierarchy list, interviewers often rank candidates' answers based on a hierarchy of impressiveness. For example, if you are interviewing for a job in the commercial industry, your strongest answers should demonstrate how you made or saved money for your previous employers. While it's important to convey your strongest highlights, avoid memorizing verbatim answers.

To make a strong impression on the interviewer, focus on highlighting your accomplishments and results in previous roles. Be prepared to provide specific examples of how you contributed to the success of your previous employers, especially in areas that are relevant to the job you are interviewing for. By showcasing your ability to make a positive impact on the company's bottom line, you can demonstrate your value as a potential employee.

How we assess candidate potential.

Employers seek candidates who have the potential to grow and improve while performing well in their current role. During the interview process, interviewers evaluate certain traits to assess a candidate's potential for growth and development. I have used the following list as my guidance in the past to determine candidate potential:

- **Motivation**

High-potential candidates possess a strong drive to excel and achieve significant accomplishments, but their goals extend beyond their individual success. They also strive for collective objectives and demonstrate humility, investing time and effort to improve their skills and abilities in all areas. This dedication to both personal and collective growth sets them apart as exceptional candidates.

- **Curiosity**

Candidates who possess a desire for personal growth tend to have a natural inclination towards exploring new experiences, seeking knowledge, and receiving honest feedback. These individuals remain open to learning and embracing change, recognizing that personal development is a continual process that requires dedication and an eagerness to expand their horizons.

- **Insight**

The capacity to gather and interpret data in a way that reveals fresh perspectives and opportunities is a valuable trait that sets candidates apart. Being able to discern patterns and connect seemingly unrelated information helps in identifying new possibilities and finding innovative solutions. This ability to gather and make sense of information is a critical skill for success in many industries.

- **Engagement**

Being able to communicate a compelling vision effectively is a highly sought-after skill by employers. Those who possess a talent for using both emotion and logic to persuade others are especially valuable. The ability to connect with people on an emotional level, while also using logic to present a clear and persuasive message, is essential for successful communication. This skill can help build strong relationships, motivate teams, and drive the achievement of shared goals.

- **Determination**

The perseverance to pursue challenging objectives in the face of obstacles and the resilience to recover from setbacks. Hiring determined candidates can bring a sense of motivation and drive to the workplace, which can inspire others to work harder and achieve more. Determination is often an indicator of a candidate's passion for their work and their commitment to producing high-quality results. This quality can also help employers identify individuals who are likely to persevere through challenges and contribute to the company's success.

Understanding the perceptions that interviewers likely have.
Interviewers may ask questions based on your resume or as a follow-up to one of your answers. Understanding how others perceive your background is key to highlighting your strengths and mitigating shortcomings. For instance, having a strong track record with a well-respected company is an advantage.

Startups often prefer candidates with experience in both established and small companies. Large organizations are known for providing comprehensive training, which can be beneficial for a candidate's next job. However, startups have a different culture, and hiring managers may prefer candidates who have previous experience in an entrepreneurial environment to ensure that they understand the culture and are a good fit.

Academic credentials from renowned institutions, such as Harvard or Stanford, can be beneficial, but they do not guarantee success. Candidates who project arrogance due to their education may not make a good impression. It is important to be self-aware and demonstrate eagerness and capability to learn.

Candidates with a history of short-term employment may be viewed with suspicion, as it may suggest issues with skills or personality. During the interview process, it is crucial to uncover any history of inferior performance or conflict with management/co-workers.

Getting some extra help – Understanding the recruiters.
When you are going through an interview process, you might work with a recruiter, either an inside/corporate recruiter or an outside/third-party recruiter, commonly referred to as a "Headhunter" for executive-level roles. Regardless of the type of recruiter you work with, there are some basic commonalities to their job, the most important being that if you impress them, they often become your advocate.

Corporate Talent Acquisition Recruiters are given goals for the number of hires they need to fill at their company, with their job performance evaluated by the metric of "Time-to-Fill". Quality-of-Hire is also tracked in many companies, including retention, performance, and promotion of employees hired by that recruiter. If you can impress the recruiter, they can become an advocate to get you hired, as it reflects well on their job performance.

Outside recruiters, including headhunters, have a direct financial incentive to become advocates for strong candidates. Most are paid on a contingency basis, meaning they only receive payment if they fill the position. If you impress an outside recruiter, they will become an advocate for you, potentially introducing you to opportunities at multiple companies.

Understanding the incentives of recruiters will help you take advantage of their assistance, and building long-term professional relationships with good recruiters can benefit your career. However, it's important to be mindful of your actions, as behaving inappropriately can damage relationships. For example, directly contacting a hiring manager without informing your recruiter can lead to negative consequences and harm your chances of future opportunities.

How to Answer Behavioral-Based
Interview Questions

Behavioral-based interview questions are based on the premise that past behavior is the best predictor of future behavior in similar situations. These questions are also known as competency-based, behavioral, situational-based, or performance-based interviews. There is a related style of questioning called skill-based interview questions. To succeed in these types of interviews, it's important to prepare in advance.

Situational-based interview questions are hypothetical, but the strongest answers are those that draw from actual experiences in comparable situations. To increase your chances of success, there is a simple exercise you can do before the interview. But before we get into that, let's cover some common advice for answering these types of questions.

Behavioral interviews are designed to test your ability to work well in various scenarios, including high-pressure situations, tight deadlines, and urgent needs. The interviewer wants to see if your decisions and attitude align with the qualities they're seeking in a candidate. You'll likely be asked to provide specific examples of times when you've been in similar situations.

To answer behavioral questions effectively, take some time to reflect on your past experiences and think about which ones are most relevant to each question. This will help you stay organized and confident during the interview. When answering, be sure to give a specific example and focus on the relevant details. Avoid providing unnecessary information that may distract from your main points.

One candidate I worked with was a borderline fit for the job on paper, but her well-prepared answers to my behavioral questions set her apart from all the other candidates. Her responses were exactly what we were looking for and she delivered them with confidence and detail. Even though the hiring manager wasn't impressed by her resume, she sailed through the rest of the process and got the job. If you want to interview successfully, follow her lead, and prepare strong examples that demonstrate the qualities the interviewer is seeking.

What is the standard advice on how to respond to behavioral-based interview questions?

Here is a list of what you can do to prepare for behavioral interview questions:

1. Examples should be tailored to the ideal profile.

2. Make a list of your previous efforts and significant achievements.

3. Formulate your answers using the STAR technique, which I will explain in this chapter.

4. Be succinct and precise in your answers.

Examples should be tailored to the ideal profile.

During a behavioral interview, it's important to remember that the interviewer is looking for specific qualities in a candidate. Your answers should provide clues that you are a good fit for the profile they're seeking. To tailor your responses to their needs, pay attention to the job description. For instance, if the position requires three years of experience and proficiency in certain software programs, you should be prepared to talk about situations where you used those programs or similar ones. By doing so, you'll show the interviewer that you have the skills they're looking for and increase your chances of landing the job.

Make a list of your previous efforts and significant achievements.

To succeed in a behavioral interview, it's crucial to spend time preparing in advance. Make a list of projects from your career that are relevant to the job you're applying for, and if you're early in your professional life, don't hesitate to use examples from your academic career if they're applicable. During the interview, be sure to include details of your experiences that demonstrate your qualifications for the job. In particular, explain how your actions led to success for your employer. If, for example, you were responsible for a significant increase in sales, be prepared to discuss the steps you took to achieve that outcome and how you can replicate that success in the future. By organizing your experiences and highlighting your achievements, you'll be well-equipped to impress the interviewer and secure the job.

Formulate your answers using the STAR technique.

The STAR technique (situation, task, action, and result) is the most popular method for answering behavioral interview questions in a clear and thorough way. Some people may refer to it as SOAR (situation, obstacle, action, and result), but it's essentially the same thing. By using this technique, you can break down your responses into easy-to-follow components that effectively convey your experience in a previous job. Each element of STAR offers a framework for telling your story when answering behavioral-based interview questions. With this technique, you'll be well-prepared to respond to questions in a way that showcases your skills and achievements and increases your chances of landing the job. Here is an explanation of each stage and an example:

- **Situation**

Describe a situation relevant to the question asked that you have faced in your work, and any essential facts the interviewer should be aware of. Prioritize pertinent information that relates to the position you are looking for.

Consider the following scenario: *"Our team had a backlog of articles that needed to be submitted and authorized by the customer in my previous job as an internal copywriter. The editors imposed strict deadlines on us in order for us to finish the items in our queue, which caused me stress."*

- **Task**

Tell the interviewer about the responsibilities that you had in this scenario. This explains the specifics of what you needed to accomplish on behalf of your former company to reach a goal. As I will explain later in the chapter, this is the least important part of the STAR technique.

"My job was to make sure that over the following five days, I produced and submitted three articles to fulfill the fifteen-article goal set by my project manager to assist the team in catching up."

- **Action**

Explain the steps that you took to meet your deadline and accomplish the objective you set for yourself. Create a list of the top talents that you want to communicate to the interviewer for this stage, which should emphasize the skill you are attempting to convey to the interviewer.

"Over the course of this period, I set up three two-hour time slots in my schedule to work on these three articles. If I had any concerns, I called the project manager, and I shut out any other distractions by listening to classical music to maintain my concentration on writing."

- **Result**

Define the results achieved due to your activities. When feasible, provide statistics or specific quantifiable outcomes and how they impacted the business at the time. You want to give a clear timeline, completion timeline, and the impact of your decisions.

"I ended up producing and submitting eight articles at the end of the week, more than double my planned goal. As a result, we were able to meet our deadline and ended up expanding our relationships with those clients."

Be succinct and precise in your answers.

When answering behavioral interview questions, it's important to keep your responses concise, ideally under two minutes. To achieve this, consider practicing with a mentor or friend who can help you focus on the main points while keeping your answers brief. Alternatively, record yourself answering the questions and listen back to assess the length and quality of your answers. Keep in mind that the interviewer may shift gears and ask different questions, so be prepared to adapt accordingly. By preparing in advance and delivering concise, relevant responses, you'll make a strong impression and increase your chances of landing the job.

Examples of Behavioral-based interview questions:

1. Describe the most challenging situation you have had to deal with in the last year.
2. Describe a moment when you exceeded your manager's expectations to help a customer.
3. Tell us about a time when a colleague needed motivation and what you did to help them.
4. Tell us about a time when your workload was a problem. What steps did you take to address this problem?
5. Have you ever felt pressured to meet a deadline? What methods did you use to deal with this problem?
6. Describe a time when you committed a blunder that had a negative impact on your team. How did you deal with that situation?
7. Tell me about a time that you had to rapidly pick up a new skill. What was the outcome, and how did you go about learning your new skill?

8. Tell me about when you had to pitch an idea to upper management. What was the outcome?

9. Have you ever had a disagreement with a coworker about the project's direction? What did you do to come to a compromise with your coworker?

Using the STAR method, here is an example of a successful behavioral-based interview answer:

Describe the most challenging situation you have had to deal with in the past year.

"I received a call from a client a year ago regarding a complaint he had about the software we provided. He stated that he wanted to cancel his account with us because the software had shut down while he was working on a critical project for his company. I asked him to take me through what had happened step by step so that I could better understand what had happened."

"After hearing his story, I decided that we should offer to refund the money he had paid for the month that the problem occurred. I called my manager and explained the situation to get her approval. Then I worked with one of our engineers to figure out the technical problem the client

had with our software. I was able to refund him the money and fix the issues with his software at no additional charge. This action resulted in retaining the account, and the consistent payments from a top client, contributing to a profit increase for my company."

This answer is successful because it takes the interviewer through a success story where you are the star of that story, and your company benefited by having you as their employee. It mostly follows the STAR method but illustrates why I am telling you that there is a more effective, and efficient method to prepare for a behavioral-based interview.

The best way to prepare to successfully answer behavioral-based interview questions.

1. Start with one or more blank sheets of paper and turn them horizontally to be in a landscape layout. (Of course, you can do this digitally if you prefer.)
2. Draw two vertical lines down the page so that you create three equal columns.
3. At the top of the left column write "Situation", center column "Action", and on the right "Results".

4. Re-read the ideal profile you wrote or the job advertisement, the duties, requirements, and any other parts that describe what the company is looking for in the person that they hire.

5. Using only bullet points, start listing specific examples from your career that relate to the ideal profile.

6. After you have put as many relevant examples as you can recall, set this page aside and when you remember another fitting example, come back to it, and jot it down. (This might take a couple of days.)

7. Once you have all the most relevant examples, re-write your page and rank them so that your best examples are listed at the top (the ones that you don't want to leave the interview without making sure you mention them.), and then list the remainder in descending order of impressiveness.

To improve your performance in behavioral-based interviews, consider using the SAR (Situation, Action, Results) technique instead of STAR (Situation, Task, Action, Results). While tasks and responsibilities are important, they're typically less significant than the situation, action, and results of your story. Focusing on these elements will make it easier to remember a greater number of examples and their details. When answering questions, start with the situation, describe the action you took, and conclude with the results you achieved. By keeping it simple and straightforward, you'll be more productive and confident.

Preparing with the SAR exercise before your interview can help you recall examples and deliver a confident, successful answer. Taking a moment to recall your list of examples, choosing the best one for the question, and sharing your success story demonstrates confidence and impresses the interviewer. Without this preparation, candidates may struggle to recall examples from their past, leading to a less confident and less impressive performance. To access this exercise and other helpful resources, check out the *COMPANION WORKBOOK: The Ultimate Guide to Successful Job Interviewing.*

Final behavioral-based interview insights.

Many candidates dislike behavioral-based interview questions because they believe they can make up stories to get hired. However, these types of questions are just one tool used to make hiring decisions. Experienced recruiters and hiring managers can spot inconsistencies and check on claims made in answers.

Candidates who are dishonest may save the interviewer time by demonstrating why they should not be hired.

The most common mistake candidates make when answering behavioral-based interview questions is to avoid answering them altogether. For example, if a candidate is asked for an example and responds with a vague non-answer like "I deal with that all the time..." or "I have many clients who do that...", they have failed to provide a specific example related to the question. After a few vague answers, most interviewers will eliminate the candidate from consideration.

Another mistake is not listening to the entire question. Candidates often focus on the example they want to use and stop listening to the interviewer. However, there may be multiple parts to the question, and candidates need to listen carefully to provide an appropriate answer.

To prepare for behavioral-based interview questions, write out bullet points for success stories and practice saying them aloud. Avoid memorizing verbatim answers and speak naturally during the interview. Remember that interview questions are chosen to determine if a candidate fits the ideal profile for the job. Answers should include examples of skills, temperament, experience, and talent that match what the company is looking for.

Canned, disingenuous answers are not recommended. Instead, memorize bullet points and speak naturally during the interview. Interviewers are also assessing personality fit, and coming across as fake or reciting answers can be detrimental to a candidate's success.

Quick reference summary:

1. Prepare ahead of time using the SAR exercise.
2. Do not make up examples.
3. Give real examples from your experience.
4. Listen to the entire question.
5. Practice saying your examples aloud before the interview.
6. Relate all your examples to the ideal profile.

Focus on the main points that you need to make.

How to Answer the Most Common Tough Interview Questions

Many job applicants have experienced the sinking feeling of being caught off-guard by unexpected or tough interview questions. While it's impossible to anticipate exactly what interviewers will ask, being familiar with common difficult questions, their purpose, and how to approach them can help job seekers feel more confident and ready.

Interview questions are designed to assess how well a candidate matches the ideal profile that an organization is looking for. For example, the classic "tell me about yourself" question has stumped many candidates. I have seen two types of candidates fail this question: the overconfident and the intimidated. Later in this chapter, I will provide tips on how to avoid these pitfalls.

Successful candidates typically prepare for tough interview questions in advance, taking the time to tailor answers to a specific organization or employer. This can make interviews go more smoothly and make applicants more impressive to interviewers. Some tough questions push candidates to think critically and creatively, while others catch candidates off guard.

No matter how challenging an interview may seem, getting hired depends on how prepared a candidate is relative to other applicants. The key is to demonstrate how well you match the job requirements and specifications. Your answers should be concise and relevant, connecting your experiences to the ideal profile.

Understanding the job and candidate profile can provide insights into the questions you may be asked during an interview. Successful interview preparation often involves practicing answering questions with a partner, recording and listening to your answers, and practicing until you are comfortable and confident. Avoid memorizing answers verbatim and instead focus on the main points you want to make and speak naturally.

Despite being a great fit on paper, I have interviewed thousands of job candidates who fell short in the interview. On the other hand, candidates who seemed less qualified on paper impressed me in the interview. To help you succeed, take a closer look at some of the most common difficult interview questions, and examples of how to answer them.

Interview questions that are difficult to answer and how to respond to them.

"Tell me about yourself."

Reason we ask: The interviewer is trying to evaluate how much of a match you are to what they want to hire. This question/statement is a quick way for us to gather certain information; do you understand the job and what we are looking for? Do you have the education and/or experience we want? For some jobs, we are evaluating your presentation skills.

Answering the open-ended question "Tell me about yourself" is an excellent chance to showcase how you align with what the interviewer is seeking. Many candidates make the mistake of giving long-winded, irrelevant answers that lack detail related to the job. For this reason, it is helpful to take a chronological approach, starting from when you began your career or education up to your current position. Your answer should be concise and no longer than 30-60 seconds, and it should include relevant achievements that demonstrate how you align with the job requirements.

When responding, you should address both the skills and personality traits required for the position. Avoid generic responses like "Unique" or "Hardworking" and instead, connect your experience, skills, and personality traits to what the employer is looking for in the ideal candidate.

Highlight specific areas where your background matches the job requirements, such as your education, experience with specific software programs or languages, or other skills that are relevant to the position. If you can, try to connect a personal trait to the company culture or the job description.

To make your answer stand out, add a brief statement that sets you apart from other candidates. Specifically, you should include your Unique Value Proposition (UVP). Your UVP should be a brief statement that clearly explains your skills, experience, and unique strengths in a way that appeals to this employer. Based on your research or knowledge about the company or industry, mention something about yourself that makes you more qualified for the job than most other candidates. To learn more about the UVP, please read my book *SoaringME The Ultimate Guide to Successful Job Searching*.

Matching your skills and personality to the ideal profile is critical in creating a strong response to this question and developing compelling positioning and closing statements. Spend time crafting a concise and powerful answer that demonstrates your ability to meet the job requirements.

What to avoid: Throughout my years of conducting interviews, I have noticed two types of candidates who consistently fail when it comes to answering the questions, "Tell me about yourself", or "Why are you a good fit for this position?" The first type is the overconfident candidate who tends to use clichés and self-promoting language without providing any evidence to back up their claims. I once had a candidate repeatedly describe themselves as an "All-star" several times during an interview without offering any examples that supported this statement. Needless to say, he did not come across as convincing and did not move forward in the interview process.

The second type of candidate who often struggles with this question is the intimidated candidate. They may not see how their skills and experiences align with the position and fail to mention them in their answer. However, it is crucial to research the job and company beforehand and identify the ways in which you are a good match. Your answer should not be about bragging but about demonstrating your qualifications for the position.

Confidence is key when answering this question. Be sure to highlight your relevant experiences and skills that make you a strong fit for the position. Avoid using generic language and provide concrete examples to support your claims. Remember, it is not just about showcasing your skills and experiences, but also about demonstrating how they align with the job requirements and company culture. By preparing and delivering a strong answer, you can stand out as a top candidate for the job.

"What are your biggest weaknesses?"

Reason we ask: Your answer to this question should tell us how self-aware you are, and if you have a weakness that makes you not compatible with the job or company.

When asked about your biggest weakness, it's important to understand that the interviewer may also phrase the question as "What is something your boss has told you that you need to work on?" or "What is one thing that you would change about yourself?" The key to answering this question is sincerity. Avoid presenting a positive trait as a flaw or mentioning a personality trait, as these responses can come across as insincere. Instead, discuss an actual professional shortcoming that you have identified, worked on, improved upon, and that will not negatively impact your performance in the job you are interviewing for. This demonstrates self-awareness and a commitment to professional growth.

Example answer of a candidate interviewing for an Executive Assistant role: *"In my previous job as a Copywriter, I lacked enough creativity to consistently produce new original content. I took workshops and I got better, but I never felt like it was what I was best at. I'm good at writing and staying organized, so I decided to find a career that was a better match for my strengths."*

The creativity needed to be a Copywriter is not required to be an exceptionally good Executive Assistant. The answer displays self-awareness and the ability to improve but does not make the interviewer doubt that the candidate is a match for the role.

What to avoid: It is crucial to avoid certain responses when asked about your biggest weakness in a job interview. The worst answer would be to claim that you do not have any weaknesses. This response portrays a lack of self-awareness and raises a red flag that you might be a difficult employee. The second-worst answer is to mention a skill from the ideal profile for the job, which could be perceived as a lack of preparation and effort. Cliché responses like "I'm a workaholic" or "I can be too driven by my work" come across as insincere and should be avoided. It's important to choose an actual professional weakness that you have identified, fixed or improved, and are continuing to work on.

"Why should I hire you over somebody else?"

Reason we ask: This answer will tell the interviewer how well you understand the job, how much of a match you are to what we want to hire, and some insight into your enthusiasm.

To prepare for "Why should I hire you over somebody else?" question, focus on practicing for "Tell me about yourself" and

"What is your greatest strength?" questions. A successful answer should demonstrate your understanding of the job and the ideal candidate profile. Provide a concise overview of how your experience and skills align with the position. Show why you are the best candidate for the job and the company without comparing yourself to others. Create a compelling and succinct explanation of why your services are valuable to the business.

Example answer for a candidate interviewing for a Data Engineer role: *"I believe that my experience lines up well with what you are looking for. My experience is directly transferable, and I have strong coding skills in both Python and R. More than just being a technical fit, I am passionate about what you're doing here and would really enjoy working on the types of projects you need done."*

What to avoid: Many candidates give a rehearsed answer to this question, which can sound artificial and insincere. It's best to avoid discussing other candidates or being negative about them, as it may indicate that you have difficulties working with others.

"Why are you interested in this job?"

Reason we ask: The answer to this question gives the interviewer insights into your career goals; how much you know about this position and company, whether you did your research, what your motivation is, how strong your motivation is, what is most important to you. All of those help us determine how much of a fit you are. Applicants who simply want any job become employees that do not stay long, and this question is an attempt to screen them out of the process.

Your response to this question should showcase that you have taken the time to research the company and the position, and that you are enthusiastic about the opportunity. While it is important to connect your background to the ideal profile, the focus of your answer should be on the company itself. Identify two or three unique attributes of the company's culture, history, products, or reputation that differentiate it from other employers. Your response should demonstrate that you are motivated, professional, and have a genuine interest in the company and the position.

Example answer:

"I'm extremely impressed with this PQRS Therapeutics reputation, and I think that your science might be the next big breakthrough. My PhD was focused on immunology, and for the past five years I have been working with Immuno-Oncology cell therapies. I think you are on the

right path with what you're developing, and I would love to be a part of advancing this type of science."

What to avoid: Mentioning compensation or benefits and displaying a lack of enthusiasm in your tone or body language are two mistakes to avoid when answering this question. Focusing too much on salary and perks can give the impression that you are not passionate about the job or the company, but only interested in what you can get out of it. Similarly, a disinterested tone or negative body language can give the impression that you are not fully invested in the opportunity, which can be a turn-off for the interviewer.

"What is your biggest achievement?"

Reason we ask: The answer to this question should give the interviewer insight into both your skills and your personality. When you choose what you consider to be your biggest achievement, it gives us insight into what you consider to be most important. Understanding what your priorities are in the workplace will help us determine if you are a good fit for our company culture. We also need a certain level of skill in the people that we hire, so understanding what you did and how well you did it for your biggest achievement will inform us about your skill-level.

Many people struggle with answering this question because they are not used to promoting themselves. However, it is a vital opportunity to showcase your accomplishments and how they align with the job you are interviewing for. Your answer should not only demonstrate an achievement but also how it could positively impact the company or team, whether it is through boosting sales or improving collaboration. Depending on the job requirements, you may also highlight your personal achievements if they show that you are a good fit. Practicing your answer beforehand can help you feel more at ease with selling yourself during the interview.

Example: The startup software company is hiring an outside sales representative. A competitive nature is a must have trait. They would prefer previous experience, but it is not required.

Answer 1: *"When I began in my current position the company had not even launched its first software program. It was a challenging start, but I built relationships with key decision makers within our target market* *and ended up winning sales representative of the year out of our team of twenty."*

Answer 2: *"I am highly driven and results-oriented, but since this will be my first professional job after graduating, I'd have to say that my greatest achievement to-date has been that I was named captain of my college soccer team three years in a row. I love what I know about your software, and I look forward to being a top performer for you, like I was in my athletic career."*

What to avoid: Do not give a vague response and instead, use a specific achievement. It's essential to be honest and avoid taking undue credit for something that was not solely your accomplishment. If you were part of a team, make sure to explain your significant contribution to the success. This answer should be backed by specific examples and not be merely a general statement. Be prepared for follow-up questions that may scrutinize your individual role in the achievement.

"What would your co-workers say about you?"

Reason we ask: Being self-aware is a particularly important soft skill for most organizations. Understanding how your behavior is perceived by others allows you to get along better with co-workers and to be more productive. Your answer to this question should give us an idea of how self-aware you are, and about your personality. We will compare your answer to all other evidence we have or observe about you. We want to see if you would be a good fit for the company culture and this question helps us make that determination.

Before the interview, take time to evaluate your own strengths and skills, and then compare them to the ideal profile that the company is seeking. Make a list of anecdotes from your work that showcase these skills. When answering this question, highlight one or at most two of your strengths that align with the job requirements. Start by telling the interviewer about these strengths and then back them up with examples from your experience.

Example answer: *"In my current role as a data engineer, most of my co-workers would describe me as a creative problem-solver. Just last quarter my team and I encountered an integration problem that we couldn't find an existing solution for. After analyzing a couple of work-around options, I presented my ideas to the team, and we worked together to solve the issues."*

This answer demonstrates both that the candidate is a creative problem-solver, but also that he/she works well within a team.

What to avoid: It's crucial to be honest while answering the interview questions. You should never fabricate skills or give false examples. The interviewers may cross-check some of your responses with others who have interviewed you. Making up skills or experiences that you do not possess is not only unprofessional but also a surefire way to lose the opportunity. **Being dishonest is the fastest and most sure-fire way to guarantee that you don't get the job.**

"What are your biggest strengths?"

Reason why we ask: This is a straightforward way for us to assess what you are best at and if that matches what we wish to hire. Your answer may also give us further insight into your personality, such as determining if you are self-aware and our view of a good fit.

The employer schedules an interview with you because they are interested in learning more about the qualities that you possess. Always keep in mind that there are other applicants competing with you for the job. It is advantageous to highlight a skill that sets you apart from other applicants, or that you excel in.

Notable strengths do not necessarily have to be hard skills; some employers are looking for the right personality that can be trained. Therefore, behavioral qualities such as tenacity or resilience might be essential when analyzing the ideal profile for the job.

When describing your greatest strength, it is important to provide evidence that supports your claim. You should give an example of a time when you displayed this strength and how it produced a positive result. A strong example that demonstrates your skill is crucial to make your answer stand out from other candidates. Lastly, your answer should tie back to the job you are interviewing for. You can simply add a brief statement at the end of your answer that explains how this strength will contribute to your success in the position.

Follow these steps to prepare for this question:

1. Make a list of your biggest strengths, experience, education, training, hard and soft skills.
2. Self-assess and rank the skills on your list or the order in which they are your strongest attributes.

3. Make a list of the desired qualities based on your understanding of the ideal profile.
4. Start with the first listed attribute that the company desires, and if it is listed as one of your top strengths, this should be the focus of your answer. If not, go to the second listed attribute on the company list. Continue until you find a genuine strength of yours that is highest on both lists.

If you can't find an overlap between the job requirements and your strengths, but you believe that one of your strengths will be valuable in this position, you must tailor your response to emphasize how this skill is relevant to the job. It's okay if you have two strengths to highlight, but keep your answer brief, lasting no more than two minutes.

Example answer: *"I have excellent organizational skills. While I was going to college full-time, I also worked twenty hours a week in the accounting department at XYZ Corp. At that job my primary responsibility was consolidation of overseas quarterly financial reports, and my boss never had to make an adjustment to any of my work. I was able to complete my accounting degree on time and graduated with honors. I know my ability to organize my time and complete projects accurately will help me be successful in this role."*

The impression this answer gives is that not only is this candidate organized, but also smart, hard-working, and motivated.

What to avoid: The way you answer this question can reveal a lot about your character and suitability for the job. Overconfidence may suggest that you are not open to constructive criticism and unwilling to improve. Conversely, being too modest may lead the interviewer to question your self-assurance and ability to excel in the role. The key is to strike a balance between confidence and humility, demonstrating that you are self-aware and coachable. Choose a strength that is specific and relevant to the job, avoiding generic or overly common answers.

"Why are you leaving your current job?" / "Why did you leave your previous job?"

Reason we ask: This question does inform us about your motivation, and whether this career move makes enough sense to lead us to believe that you will be a long-term employee for us. But the tricky part of this question is how much we can learn about your personality.

Complaining about your current or previous job, colleagues, or bosses during an interview can leave a negative impression on potential employers, even if your complaints are genuine. Instead, focus on what you want to achieve in your next career step and match those desires with what the new job offers. Always try to relate your answer back to how you are a good fit for the opportunity. The approach to answering this question might differ depending on how you left your previous employment. Therefore, I am providing some scenarios and example answers to guide you.

Example answer for someone who voluntarily left/are leaving on good terms with their employer:

"I am grateful for the opportunity that I had at ABC Company, it was a wonderful experience but it's just time for me to take on a new challenge and show that I can accomplish even more than I already have. Your company will provide me with the opportunity to do that."

Example answer for someone who voluntarily left/are leaving on less than good terms with their employer:

"I learned a lot in my time with ABC Company, but over time I realized what I really need is an opportunity that is going to both challenge me and allow me to work with a product that I can be passionate about. I really like what I've learned about your company and products. This is a better fit for me and where I want to take my career."

Example answers for someone who was laid-off by their employer not due to performance:

"Unfortunately, my company went through a re-structuring in April. Since I was one of the most recent hires, I was part of a group that was let go. I have received an above average performance review, and my manager will be one of my references. The work that I had done well in that position is very similar to your position so I'm confident I will get up to speed very quickly."

Example answer for someone who was terminated by their employer:

"When I was originally hired it was because they were looking to bring a different skill set into ABC Company. I made appropriate changes and we did increase sales by 33%, but it quickly became clear that the President and I have different styles. I learned that to thrive, I need an innovative and collaborative environment, which is exactly what I see that your company promotes itself to be."

Notice that this answer is not negative towards the previous employer or boss, makes the point that at least some of the work done was good, and brings it all back to being a good fit for this new job. It does not give every detail about being fired and does not tell a lie. You should expect follow-up questions about some of the details, but continue to be concise, honest, positive, and professional. If you made a mistake at your previous job, explain how you have learned from it and why it will not be a problem for your next employer.

What to avoid: It is not appropriate to share negative experiences or personal conflicts with previous employers during an interview. Over-explaining or becoming emotional about your reasons for leaving a previous job should be avoided as well. Honesty is important, but it is never acceptable to lie about how you left a previous job. Remember that background checks are typically conducted, and if dishonesty is discovered, it could lead to termination from the new job.

"What are your salary expectations?"
(See the later chapter entitled *The Job Offer*.)

Common Interview Questions for BioPharmaceutial Sales Jobs

When evaluating candidates for biopharma sales positions, I take into account several factors beyond their answers to my questions. At the start of the interview, I often pose an open-ended question such as "Tell me about yourself," "Provide an overview of your background," or "Give me a highlight reel of your experience." Then, I pay close attention to the candidate's performance and presentation skills. Their ability to present their answers concisely and impactfully is a crucial indicator of their potential success when presenting to physicians. The way they present themselves also reveals their ability to deliver persuasive presentations and their communication style. I assess whether they can articulate their points in a concise and focused manner in a way that would engage and persuade a doctor. Additionally, the substance of their answers provides me with insight into their experience with different call points and settings. I typically follow up with questions about their sales rankings, results, and any awards they've received.

At the end of the interview, I carefully observe whether the candidate attempts to close and move onto the next step in the interview process or asks a closing question. This is an important indication of their ability to confidently and effectively close sales, a vital skill in the biotech/pharma sales industry.

When evaluating entry-level candidates for biopharmaceutical sales roles, I prioritize their skillset and ability to absorb and retain technical information. While they prefer candidate that have at least prior B2B sales experience, many employers in this industry are willing to train new hires who show potential and possess the basic skills necessary for success. Therefore, my focus is on assessing whether these entry-level candidates possess transferrable skills that are essential to the role, including being driven, persuasive, capable of learning technical information, skilled in building relationships, well-organized, and resilient. These skills are critical for success in the biopharmaceutical sales industry, and I look for evidence of their presence in the candidate's background, experience, and demeanor during the interview process.

In contrast, when considering candidates for more senior roles, such as hospital or therapeutic specialty positions, I place greater emphasis on their past biopharmaceutical sales track record. My clients typically seek candidates with a consistent history of top-tier sales performance, ranking in the top 20-25% of their sales force. The most desirable candidates have a track record of ranking in the top 10% and have won multiple sales awards.

In addition to past performance, most biopharmaceutical employers prefer candidates who already have strong relationships with the hospitals or specialist physicians that the role they are hiring for will call on. While this is a preferred trait, a highly qualified candidate without pre-existing relationships will be chosen over an average candidate who does have those relationships. Ultimately, a strong sales track record is the most important factor for candidates seeking senior-level biopharmaceutical sales roles.

Common entry-level biopharma sales interview questions:

"What do you know about the roles of a biotech or pharmaceutical sales representative?"

Reason we ask: This question gives the interviewer insight into whether you have done your research and are genuinely interested in the job and the industry. BioPharmaceutical companies invest a significant amount of time and resources into training their sales representatives, making it crucial for them to carefully evaluate potential hires to ensure they are a smart long-term investment.

When asked about the roles of a biotech or pharmaceutical sales representative, it's important to show that you have researched the industry and understand the responsibilities of the job. A good answer would include a description of the primary duties of a sales representative, such as promoting and selling products to healthcare professionals, building and maintaining relationships with key physicians, and staying up to date with the latest industry trends and developments.

Example answer: "I understand that a pharmaceutical sales representative is responsible for promoting and selling products to healthcare professionals, such as doctors and pharmacists. They need to be knowledgeable about the products they sell and able to communicate the benefits to the prescribing physicians. They also need to stay up to date with the latest industry trends and developments to provide the best possible service to customers."

This answer shows that the candidate has done their research and has a good understanding of the primary duties of a sales representative in the biotech or pharmaceutical industry.

What to avoid: It's important to avoid giving generic or incorrect responses that show a lack of knowledge or preparation. Responses like "I don't know much about the industry" or "I think it's selling drugs to pharmacies" could disqualify you from consideration. Similarly, avoid making assumptions about the industry or the job responsibilities without doing your research. It's important to be specific and demonstrate your knowledge of the industry and the job role.

"Tell me about your previous sales experience. How were you so successful?"

Reason we ask: This question helps us evaluate your previous sales experience, and if those experiences are transferable to the BioPharmaceutical industry. It gives insight into the strategies you used, and the results you achieved. We want to know if you can articulate your sales process, adapt to different situations, and if your experience aligns with the job you are interviewing for.

When answering this question, it's essential to give specific examples of your previous sales experience and the strategies you used to achieve success. Your answer should demonstrate your sales process, communication skills, problem-solving abilities, and ability to close deals. Transferable skills are building relationships with a decision-maker and their staff, selling technical products, and managing a territory.

Example answer: ""In my previous role as a technology solutions sales representative, I was responsible for selling complex software and hardware products to businesses across various industries. Effective communication of technical information was crucial in this role, as I needed to articulate the benefits of our products to a range of audiences, including IT professionals, procurement managers, and C-suite executives.

To succeed in this role, I made a conscious effort to understand the unique needs and pain points of each of my clients. I researched their businesses and industries thoroughly, and I tailored my approach to each client to ensure that I addressed their specific concerns. Building strong relationships with my clients was essential to building trust and credibility, and I made sure to follow up with them regularly to ensure their satisfaction with our products and services.

In addition to building relationships, I also managed a large territory, which required strong organizational and time-management skills. I created and executed a comprehensive sales plan that allowed me to prioritize my clients and maximize my efficiency in the field. This included regularly scheduling meetings with key decision-makers, providing ongoing support to existing clients, and prospecting for new business opportunities.

By focusing on building relationships, selling technical products, and managing my territory effectively, I was able to consistently exceed my sales targets and grow my client base."

This answer shows that the candidate has a clear understanding of their sales process and strategies, including research, tailoring their approach to different audiences, and building strong relationships with clients.

What to avoid: It's essential to avoid giving vague or general responses about your previous sales experience. Avoid making claims about your success without providing any specific examples or details. It's also important to avoid talking negatively about your previous employers or clients, as this can raise red flags about your professionalism and attitude. Finally, avoid discussing sales experience that is not directly relevant to the job you are interviewing for, as this may not demonstrate your ability to adapt to the specific industry or products/services.

"Tell me about a time that you had to get past the gatekeepers in order to build a relationship with the decision maker."

Reason we ask: This question is intended to gauge your sales skills, persistence, and ability to build relationships with key decision-makers. It is important to understand how you approach challenges in the sales process and if you can effectively navigate obstacles to achieve your goals.

Example answer: "In my previous job as a sales rep for a medical supply company, I was tasked with building a relationship with a key decision-maker in a hospital. However, I found that there were several gatekeepers who were hesitant to let me through to speak with the decision-maker. Rather than giving up, I focused on building relationships with the gatekeepers themselves, learning about their work and showing a genuine interest in their roles. Over time, I was able to establish trust and credibility with them, and they began to introduce me to the decision-maker.

Eventually, I was able to build a strong relationship with the decision-maker, which led to a successful partnership with the hospital."

This answer shows the candidate's persistence, communication skills, and ability to build relationships, which are all important qualities for a sales representative. Additionally, it demonstrates the candidate's ability to adapt their approach and find creative solutions to overcome obstacles.

What to avoid: When answering this question, it is important to avoid responses that paint you in a negative light, such as blaming the gatekeepers or the decision-maker for any failures. It is also important to avoid responses that lack detail or specifics, as these can make it difficult for the interviewer to understand your approach and effectiveness. Finally, avoid responses that show a lack of persistence or give up easily when faced with obstacles, as this is not a desirable trait in a sales role.

"How do you stay up to date with the latest advances in your current industry?"

Reason we ask: This question is asked to determine how committed you are to professional development and keeping up with the latest trends in your industry. Employers want to know that you have a genuine interest in staying informed and are willing to invest your time and effort in improving your skills and knowledge.

Example answer: "I stay up to date with the latest advances in my industry by attending conferences, workshops, and webinars. I also read industry-specific publications and follow thought leaders on social media. I believe that staying informed on the latest trends is crucial to creating effective marketing strategies and campaigns."

This answer demonstrates the candidate's proactive approach to staying informed and the importance they place on staying up to date with the latest advances in their industry.

What to avoid: It's important to avoid giving a vague or non-specific answer, such as "I just stay informed through my job" or "I keep up with the latest advances through my colleagues." This suggests a lack of effort and interest in professional development. Also, avoid mentioning outdated sources of information or not being able to provide any concrete examples of how you stay informed.

"What's your biggest sales success?"

Reason we ask: This question helps the interviewer understand your experience and achievements in sales, giving them an idea of what you can bring to the role. Your answer can demonstrate your abilities, sales techniques, and approach to handling challenges.

Example answer: "In my previous role as a territory sales representative, I was able to lead my company in launch of their new product by achieving sales of 50% over goal. I achieved this success by researching and identifying key decision-makers, building relationships with gatekeepers, and presenting the product's unique value proposition. I also worked closely with my team to ensure a smooth implementation process for our customers."

This answer demonstrates the candidate's ability to research, strategize, build relationships, and work collaboratively to achieve sales success.

What to avoid: Avoid exaggerating or fabricating your sales success. Be honest and transparent about your experiences and achievements. We often double check these types of answers. Also, avoid taking sole credit for any sales success as sales is usually a team effort. Instead, acknowledge the contributions of your team and highlight your specific role in the process.

"What are your long-term career goals?"

Reason we ask: This question allows the interviewer to understand your motivation and whether your goals align with the company's goals. It also shows your commitment to your career development and your ability to plan for the future.

Example answer: "My long-term goal is to become a top-performing sales representative in the biopharma industry, where I can contribute to the growth and success of the company. I plan to achieve this by continuously learning about the latest developments in the industry, honing my sales skills, and building strong relationships with key decision-makers. As I progress in my career, I would like to take on leadership roles within the company and mentor new hires to help them achieve their goals."

This answer shows a clear understanding of the biopharma industry and the importance of staying current with industry advancements. It also demonstrates the candidate's ambition and their desire to advance their career within the company.

What to avoid: It's important to avoid vague or unrealistic goals that don't align with the position or the company. Avoid mentioning goals that could be perceived as stepping stones to leaving the company, such as starting your own business. It's also best to avoid mentioning goals that are not relevant to the position you are applying for, such as wanting to become a researcher when applying for a sales role.

Common interview questions for senior/specialty/hospital biopharma sales roles:

"How has your previous sales performance been? Do you know your sales ranking?"

Reason we ask: We ask this question to understand how successful you have been in your previous sales roles and if you have a track record of exceeding sales targets. We also want to know if you are competitive and results-oriented and how well you can quantify your achievements.

Example answer: "In my last role, I consistently exceeded my sales targets and was ranked in the top 10% of the sales team. I attribute my success to my ability to build strong relationships with clients and really understand their needs. I also stay up to date with industry trends and am always looking for ways to improve my sales techniques."

This answer demonstrates the candidate's ability to meet or exceed sales targets, build strong relationships with clients, and continuously improve their sales skills.

What to avoid: It is important to avoid giving vague or general answers such as "I did well in my previous sales roles." Instead, provide specific numbers and details that quantify your achievements. It is also important to avoid being overly boastful or arrogant when discussing your sales success. While it's important to demonstrate your competitive and results-oriented nature, be sure to do so in a humble and professional manner. One pet peeve of mine is when candidates take credit for great sales results that happen in their first six months or so in the territory. In pharmaceutical sales as with many B2B sales, those results are due to the person who was in the territory prior to this candidate being in the job. Lastly, if your sales performance was not as strong as you would have liked, be honest about it but also explain what you learned from the experience and how you plan to improve in your next role.

"Did you work in a sales POD? How do you measure your individual contributions?"

Reason we ask: In the biopharma industry, sales performance is crucial. Asking this question helps the interviewer understand how you have contributed to your team's success and whether you have experience working collaboratively in a POD. It also assesses your ability to measure your own individual success.

Example answer: "Yes, I worked in a sales POD for the past three years. Our POD consisted of five sales representatives, and we were each responsible for all the primary care physicians within our specific territory. To measure my individual contributions, I set personal goals for each quarter, such as the number of new offices I was able to add to my calls, increasing my territory's sales by a certain percentage or closing a specific number of deals. I also tracked my progress on a weekly basis and discussed my results with my manager during our one-on-one meetings."

This answer shows that the candidate has experience working in a team environment and is proactive in setting and achieving their individual goals. The candidate also demonstrates their ability to track their own performance and communicate it to their manager.

What to avoid: Avoid giving a vague or non-specific answer. Also, avoid taking full credit for team success. The interviewer wants to understand how you contributed to the team's success, but they also don't want to see that you are a team player who takes undo credit for the sales success that was a team effort. Avoid saying that you do not measure your individual contributions or that you do not believe in setting goals, as this may come across as unambitious or lacking in accountability.

"How do you use data to improve the results in your current territory?"

Reason we ask: Sales roles in the biopharma industry are heavily data-driven, and success depends on the ability to analyze and utilize data effectively. This question aims to understand your approach to data analysis and how you use it to drive results.

Example answer: "I have a rigorous approach to data analysis and use it to inform my sales strategy. I regularly review my territory's sales data, identify trends, and analyze gaps to identify opportunities for growth. For example, in my previous role, I noticed a decrease in sales for a particular product in my territory. I dug into the data and discovered that our product was losing market share to a competitor. I developed a targeted campaign to address this, focusing on the features that set our product apart and highlighting our strengths over the competition. As a result, we were able to increase sales and regain our market share."

What to avoid: Avoid over-reliance on data without considering other factors, such as customer feedback and market trends. Make sure to emphasize your ability to interpret and apply data in a meaningful way to drive sales results. Data is meant to increase the consistency of successful sales results, so avoid any answer that does not demonstrate a strong understanding of the data and how to use it properly.

"Tell me about the most challenging doctor or clinic that you've called on."

Reason we ask: This question helps the interviewer to assess your sales skills and ability to handle difficult situations. The response will give insight into how you approach obstacles and how you manage professional relationships.

Example answer: "I remember calling on a specialist clinic where the physician was averse to trying new treatments. It was a challenge to establish trust with the physician, and it took me several calls and conversations with him to understand his concerns and how our product could help his patients. I worked with our medical team to provide clinical data and studies, and eventually, we were able to secure the clinic's business."

This response demonstrates the candidate's ability to handle difficult customers and their willingness to collaborate with different teams to achieve their goals. The answer also shows the candidate's persistence and problem-solving skills.

What to avoid: Avoid mentioning any specific details that could violate patient privacy or discussing any negative comments or gossip about a particular doctor or clinic. It's also important to avoid sounding defensive or negative about the experience. Instead, focus on the steps you took to address the challenge and how you overcame it.

"What is your favorite therapeutic area?"

Reason we ask: Asking about a candidate's favorite therapeutic area can help the interviewer gauge the candidate's level of interest and passion for a specific area of medicine. This can also help the interviewer understand the candidate's expertise, experience, and suitability for the role. Candidates who have a passion for the same or a closely related therapeutic area are a great long-term investment, those who have a strong passion for a different therapeutic area are likely to leave if a new job opportunity becomes available in that specialty area.

Example answer: "My favorite therapeutic area is oncology. I have always been fascinated by the complexity of cancer and the challenges that it presents in terms of treatment. In my current role, I have focused on developing deep expertise in oncology and building relationships with key stakeholders in the field. This has enabled me to consistently exceed my sales targets and drive meaningful impact for patients."

This answer demonstrates the candidate's passion for a specific therapeutic area and their ability to leverage their expertise to drive sales results.

What to avoid: It's important to avoid giving a generic or non-specific answer to this question. For example, saying that you have no preference or that you enjoy all therapeutic areas may come across as disinterested or lacking in expertise. Additionally, be careful not to overstate your level of knowledge or experience in a specific therapeutic area, as this can be easily detected during the interview process. Avoid showing a strong preference for a therapeutic area that is different from the position you are interviewing for.

Common interview questions for frontline biopharma sales managers:

"Can you give an example of how you have developed and mentored team members in the past?"

Reason we ask: This question aims to understand your ability to develop and mentor your team, which is a critical skill for biopharma sales managers.

As a first-time sales manager candidate, it's important to have prior experience in developing and mentoring team members. When answering this question, highlight a specific example of how you mentored a team member and helped them achieve their goals. Start by outlining the team member's strengths and areas for improvement, then discuss the steps you took to support them, such as providing regular feedback, coaching them on specific skills, and setting achievable goals.

Example answer: "As a Team Leader in my previous role, I had the opportunity to mentor and develop team members, which gave me valuable experience in managing and coaching individuals. One team member in particular was struggling with handling difficult physicians, and after identifying her strengths in other areas, I realized that a lack of confidence was the root cause of her difficulty.

To help her improve, I provided additional training and support, including role-playing exercises and one-on-one coaching sessions. I also provided regular feedback and constructive criticism to help her develop her skills and build her confidence. Over time, her confidence grew, and she was able to handle difficult calls with ease.

My approach to coaching and mentoring proved successful, resulting in a 20% increase in scripts for her territory. This experience taught me the importance of identifying individual strengths and weaknesses, providing targeted support and training, and regularly providing feedback and coaching to develop skills and build confidence. I believe that these skills are transferable to a biopharma sales management role, where I can use my experience to develop and motivate a sales team to achieve their goals and exceed expectations."

What to avoid: Avoid providing a generic answer that does not demonstrate a clear understanding of the skills required for mentoring and developing team members. Avoid mentioning a situation where you did not successfully mentor someone or one where you made a significant mistake that impacted the team member negatively. Instead, focus on a specific example where you were successful in mentoring and developing a team member. Lastly, do not take full credit for the team member's success, as it could come across as arrogant. It's essential to highlight the team members' hard work and dedication as well.

"Tell me what your priorities would be in your first 90 days in the job."

Reason we ask: This question is designed to gauge your ability to set priorities, plan and execute on those plans. As a frontline biopharma sales manager, it's essential that you can identify the most important tasks that need to be completed in the first 90 days to ensure success in the role.

Example answer: "In my first 90 days in this role, my priority would be to get to know my team and understand their strengths, weaknesses, and areas of opportunity. I would also spend time reviewing the current sales processes and tools to identify areas for improvement. Additionally, I would prioritize building strong relationships with key stakeholders, such as KOLs, and identify potential opportunities for growth in the marketplace. Finally, I would create a comprehensive sales plan for the next quarter, aligning with the company's goals and strategies, and ensure that my team is fully prepared and equipped to execute on that plan."

This answer demonstrates the candidate's ability to prioritize tasks, work collaboratively with their team and stakeholders, and take a strategic approach to achieving their goals.

What to avoid: Avoid giving a generic answer, such as "my priority would be to learn about the company and its culture." This response does not demonstrate that you understand the specific requirements of the role and the industry. Additionally, avoid mentioning tasks that are not relevant to the job or company. For example, if you are interviewing for a frontline biopharma sales manager role, do not mention tasks related to finance or human resources. Finally, avoid coming across as overly confident or unrealistic. Make sure your priorities are achievable and that you are willing to seek feedback and adjust your plans as needed.

"What is your vision for how you will make your next team successful?"

Reason we ask: This question aims to assess your leadership and management skills, as well as your ability to develop and execute a strategic plan for a team. Your answer should demonstrate your ability to motivate and develop a team, set clear goals, and establish priorities.

Example answer: "My vision is to create a culture of accountability, collaboration, and excellence in our team. I would start by getting to know each team member, understanding their strengths and weaknesses, and aligning their skills to the company's goals. I believe in setting clear expectations and objectives, regularly checking in with the team, and providing constructive feedback to foster growth. In addition, I would prioritize communication and collaboration, creating opportunities for the team to share knowledge and ideas. Finally, I would ensure that the team has the necessary resources and training to execute the strategic plan effectively."

This answer highlights the candidate's leadership style, values, and strategy, and shows that they have a clear plan to develop and lead a successful team.

What to avoid: Avoid providing generic or vague answers that do not demonstrate your leadership capabilities or strategic thinking. For instance, saying that you will "motivate the team" or "focus on results" without providing specific steps or goals can be seen as lacking direction or vision. Also, avoid making unrealistic or grandiose statements that are not supported by facts or experience. Lastly, do not disparage or criticize past teams or managers, as this can demonstrate a lack of professionalism and teamwork.

"How do you use analytics to drive performance?"

Reason we ask: As a frontline biopharma sales manager, your ability to analyze data and use it to drive performance is critical. Your answer to this question will help us understand how you approach data analysis and how you use data to drive results.

Example answer: "As a sales manager, I understand the importance of analyzing data to make informed decisions. I regularly use data to identify trends and patterns in market behavior, track the performance of my team and make strategic decisions that drive revenue growth. For example, in my previous role, I identified a trend in customer behavior that showed a significant increase in demand for a particular product. I shared this information with my team and created a sales campaign around this product, resulting in a significant increase in sales. I also use data to identify areas where my team needs improvement, such as low scripts or lack of access, and develop training programs to address these issues."

What to avoid: When answering this question, avoid making sweeping statements about your data analysis skills without providing specific examples to back them up. Similarly, avoid mentioning the use of analytics without providing a clear explanation of how you have used analytics in the past to achieve specific results. It's also important to avoid overstating your data analysis skills or using technical jargon that the interviewer may not understand. Instead, provide clear and specific examples of how you have used analytics to drive results in previous roles.

"How do you decide the way you divide your time between your different representatives?"

Reason we ask: As a frontline biopharma sales manager, it's important to be able to effectively allocate your time and resources to your team members in a fair and balanced way. This question aims to assess your ability to prioritize, delegate, and manage your team's performance.

Example answer: "When it comes to dividing my time between my representatives, I prioritize based on each rep's individual needs and performance. I take into account factors such as their current sales goals, their previous performance, and any areas where they may need additional coaching or support. I also make sure to allocate my time fairly, so that each rep feels supported and valued. I communicate regularly with each of my reps to ensure that I'm meeting their needs and that we're working together to achieve their goals."

This answer shows that the candidate has a systematic approach to time management, is responsive to the needs of their team, and values open communication.

What to avoid: It's important to avoid answers that suggest that you prioritize one representative over another or that you neglect certain team members. This can indicate favoritism or a lack of leadership skills. It's also important to avoid answers that show that you lack a clear system for managing your team's performance, as this can indicate a lack of organization or attention to detail. Additionally, avoid giving vague or non-specific answers, as this can suggest a lack of confidence or experience in managing a team.

"Tell me about a time that you had to address a performance issue with someone on your team."

Reason we ask: As a frontline biopharma sales manager, you will be responsible for managing a team of sales representatives. This question helps us assess your ability to handle difficult conversations and provide constructive feedback to improve performance. We want to know how you approach coaching and mentoring team members to achieve their goals and meet the company's objectives.

Example answer: "In my previous role as a sales manager, I had a team member who was consistently falling short of their sales targets. I scheduled a one-on-one meeting with them to discuss their performance, and we reviewed their sales data and analyzed their approach to customer engagement. We identified several areas where they could improve, such as asking more open-ended questions and actively listening to the customer's needs. I provided them with some training and resources to help them improve their sales skills and set some clear performance goals for the upcoming quarter. Over the next few months, I provided regular feedback and coaching to help them stay on track, and by the end of the quarter, they had exceeded their sales target."

This answer demonstrates the candidate's ability to approach performance issues proactively, identify the root causes of underperformance, provide constructive feedback and coaching, and collaborate with their team members to create a plan for improvement.

What to avoid: Avoid discussing a performance issue in a negative light, such as blaming the team member or focusing only on their mistakes. Also, avoid being too vague or general when describing your approach to addressing performance issues. It's important to provide specific examples and highlight the outcome of your efforts to demonstrate your effectiveness as a leader.

The Do's and Don'ts of Interviewing

There are a few key factors that can make or break your success in any interview process. To help you out, I've put together a list of these factors for you to review and keep in mind.

Things that you should do if you want to be more successful in your interviews.

Do thorough research before your interview.
To succeed in the interview, you need to prepare yourself by doing thorough research. Start by gathering as much information as possible about the company, their mission, and how the position you are interviewing for will contribute to achieving their goals. Additionally, familiarize yourself with the industry and who their main competitors are. To prepare for the specific job, study the job description, identify what qualities the ideal candidate should have, and think of ways to highlight your

strengths that align with those qualities. It is also beneficial to conduct social media research on the interviewers, as this can provide valuable insights into their background and interests. By learning about them, you can also prepare thoughtful questions to ask during the interview.

Prepare in advance.

Try to plan and prepare for your interview in advance so that you don't feel rushed or stressed out. It's essential to stay calm and relaxed in the hours leading up to your interview. Take some time to unwind and listen to something uplifting that puts you in a positive state of mind. Strive to be professional, but also friendly and approachable, as the hiring team will be evaluating your personality and attitude as well as your qualifications and experience.

Dress for the job you are interviewing for.

When preparing for your interview, consider the dress code for the job you want, and aim to dress at least one level above that standard. Remember, the version of you that the interviewer sees during the interview should be your best self. Dressing inappropriately, such as wearing jeans and a t-shirt to an interview for a business-casual job, shows a lack of understanding and interest in the position.

Focus on your accomplishments more than your duties.

As previously discussed in this book, the answers you provide during an interview hold a hierarchy of impressiveness. While a candidate may possess all the necessary skills for the job, providing weak answers can still leave a negative impression on the interviewer.

Include transferable skills if you are newly graduated or doing a career change.

If you do not have direct accomplishments or experience, use things that you have done that transfer well to the profile.

Express interest and enthusiasm for the opportunity.

A common mistake that candidates make is not being sure if they genuinely want the position, and this lack of commitment shows in their demeanor during the interview. If you are interviewing for a job, it is important to convey your interest in the position and make a positive impression. Ultimately, you want the decision to be yours to make. If you are offered the job and decide it is not the right career move, that is okay, as it will be your decision. However, if you come across as indifferent during the interview, the interviewer may decide that you are not the right fit for the job. Towards the end of the interview, show your interest by asking about the next steps and expressing what you like about the company and the opportunity.

Have good eye-contact and body language.

Showing lack of presence during an interview indicates a lack of interest, enthusiasm, and professionalism. This type of behavior can hinder your chances of being hired, as employers prefer candidates who show genuine interest and enthusiasm. Being disinterested and indifferent may suggest that you are only looking for a short-term position and not committed to doing high-quality work. So, it is crucial to stay engaged and present throughout the interview to make a positive impression.

Listen carefully to each question, even clarify what the interviewer is asking if needed.

Being mentally present during an interview is crucial for a candidate to succeed. It's common to get lost in your own thoughts and focus on what you're going to say next, but failing to pay attention to the interviewer's question can result in a poor answer. This not only reflects a lack of listening skills but also shows a lack of interest in the job and the interview process. To avoid this mistake, listen carefully to the question and take a moment to gather your thoughts before answering.

Answer all questions but use Answer/Ask.

The most impressive candidates are often those who exude a relaxed and confident demeanor during interviews. This book can help you achieve that. A candidate who engages in a back-and-forth conversation with the interviewer is more memorable than those who simply answer questions. When you ask questions, make sure they are relevant to the topic at hand. For example, if the interviewer asks about your preferred technology, you can answer and follow up by asking the interviewer about their preferences. Practice this technique of answering and then asking with someone beforehand and aim to use it about thirty percent of the time. This approach not only makes you stand out from other candidates, but it also helps you learn more about the job opportunity.

Example: Interviewer asks you *"What CRM software do you have experience with?"* and you respond with *"I have worked mostly with Salesforce, HubSpot, and Keap. What CRM do you use here and how do you like it?"*

Practice before your interview.

Rather than memorizing your answers, practice articulating your main points confidently. A helpful technique is recording yourself leaving your answers in your own voicemail and then listening to them later for self-reflection. Alternatively, consider finding a friend or colleague to conduct "mock interviews" with you. One effective exercise is to play the role of the interviewer and ask questions based on the ideal candidate profile to determine whether they would be a good fit. Through this process, you can gain valuable insights into areas you need to improve upon in your own answers.

Send a thank you email or note after every interview.

Sending a thank you note after your interview is a great way to show your appreciation and leave a positive impression. It is recommended to send the thank you note within 24 hours of the interview or one day before the interviewer makes their decision if they have specified a date. An email is usually the best way to send the note, but if the industry is more personal, a physical note may be more appropriate. If you do not have the interviewer's email, you can send it to the recruiter and ask them to forward it to the interviewer on your behalf.

Follow-up thank you email/notes should be short, typically 3-4 sentences long and should include:

1. Thank the interviewer for their time.

2. Remind them of the top 1 or 2 things about your fit for the job that you believe impressed them.

3. If needed, try to mitigate any concerns about your fit with the job that they expressed. (One sentence.)

4. Convey interest in moving forward with the interview process or receiving an offer for the job.

Accept that this is a process, and you will not get every job that you want.

Perseverance is key in the job interview process. Even if you have a less than perfect interview, it is important to stay positive and learn from your mistakes. Take an honest look at your performance and make small adjustments to improve your approach. It can be challenging, but keeping a positive attitude is essential for success.

I recall working with a recent college graduate who had no professional experience, but was determined to become a pharmaceutical sales representative. She had some social awkwardness but was likable and eager to learn. While she was not a top candidate, I believed in her and arranged for her to interview with two of my clients. Despite not receiving an offer, she persevered and continued to interview on her own. Eventually, she landed a job with a major company and has spent over two decades in her desired career. With each interview, she gained more confidence and improved her approach.

Remember to stay persistent, remain positive, and keep working at it. Even if you face rejection or setbacks, every interview is a learning opportunity to help you become a better candidate.

Things that you should avoid if you want to be more successful in your interviews:

Forgetting something.

Allow yourself ample time to prepare for your interview. This will help you avoid any last-minute mishaps and ensure that you do not forget anything important. Before your interview, the hiring manager may request that you review specific information, complete a questionnaire, or undertake an assignment. Make sure you have completed all these tasks before your interview. It is important to double- and triple-check everything to ensure you don't miss anything important.

Arriving late.

When it comes to face-to-face interviews, it's best to arrive at the location ten to fifteen minutes before your scheduled interview time. However, for phone or video interviews, make sure to be ready three to five minutes before the scheduled time, whether it's logging in to a video platform or having your phone nearby and fully charged.

No call/no show.

Failing to show up for your interview without any notice, especially through a phone call, is a surefire way to miss out on a job opportunity. It can have a long-lasting negative impact on your reputation, not only for the job in question but also for future opportunities. This kind of behavior is unprofessional and can lead to a lasting negative impression, which may harm your chances of securing the position you desire."

Sounding as though your answers are just rehearsed words you think you are supposed to say.

Although it is important to prepare for expected interview questions, it is equally important to avoid appearing too rehearsed. Instead of memorizing responses word-for-word, focus on bullet points you want to cover in your answers.

Practicing ahead of time is helpful, but try to strike a balance between preparedness and spontaneity. Being sincere and relaxed during the interview will go a long way in impressing your interviewer.

Leave your phone volume on during the interview.

Although it may seem like a small detail, forgetting to silence your phone during an interview can have a negative impact on your candidacy. While it may not be a dealbreaker, it could make a difference if another candidate is equally qualified. It may come across as unprofessional and suggest that you lack attention to detail. Therefore, make sure to double-check that your phone is silenced before the interview to avoid any potential distractions or interruptions.

Speaking negatively about previous jobs.

When interviewing for a job, it's important to maintain a positive attitude and avoid speaking negatively about previous employers or colleagues. Complaining or gossiping may lead the interviewer to perceive you as a toxic ex-employee. Instead, focus on your accomplishments, objectives, and connections. If asked about a bad experience, frame it as a learning opportunity. Highlight your interest in the new company and how your skills and experiences align with their goals. This positive approach will make you a more attractive candidate and increase your chances of success.

Being arrogant or rude to anyone.

It's crucial to be courteous and friendly to everyone you encounter while interviewing at a company. Remember, the interviewer might ask for feedback from any staff member you interacted with during your visit. Therefore, it's crucial to be polite and kind to all employees, from the receptionist to the janitor. It's also an excellent opportunity to demonstrate your interpersonal skills, as being pleasant and engaging with people you meet can give the interviewer a positive impression of you.

Being dishonest.

Lying or even appearing dishonest can be an automatic dealbreaker, even if you have all the qualifications. Employers have ways of verifying information, and if they find out you've lied, it's game over. Even if you somehow manage to get hired, any dishonesty that is later uncovered can lead to termination. It's always better to be honest, even if it means admitting a weakness or a lack of experience in a certain area.

Delay in responding to recruiters or hiring managers.

Feedback is crucial after an interview with someone besides the recruiter. Hiring managers and recruiters may also request clarification on something you mentioned during an interview. Failing to provide timely responses or withholding information gives the impression that you are not motivated to get the job. It is important to provide requested information promptly and with transparency.

Over-explaining.

When answering interview questions, it's important to be concise and to the point. A good rule of thumb is to keep your responses to about thirty to sixty seconds. If your answer goes over ninety seconds, it may be too long and lose the interviewer's attention. Try to avoid meandering or rambling answers. If the interviewer wants more detail or clarification, they will ask follow-up questions. Remember to be concise and clear while still answering the question that is being asked.

Giving vague answers.

When answering interview questions, make sure to provide specific examples to support your responses. Vague answers can come across as evasive, and can give the impression that you are trying to hide something or are not being truthful. Remember, the interviewer is trying to assess your skills and experience, so providing concrete examples helps to demonstrate your qualifications and build credibility. Avoid giving general or overly broad responses, and instead provide details that highlight your strengths and accomplishments.

Demonstrating a lack of taking responsibility.

When discussing past mistakes, avoid blaming others. During an interview, you may be asked to talk about a time when you made a mistake at work. It's important to take ownership of your actions and avoid placing the blame solely on your colleagues. Claiming that you've never made a mistake may come across as insincere. Instead, talk about what you learned from the mistake and how you would handle the situation differently if it were to happen again.

Don't get the most out of your time.

It's important to remember that interviews are not just about answering questions but also about asking them. If you only focus on answering questions and do not ask any, it can leave a negative impression on the interviewer. Research the company beforehand and prepare a list of questions to ask. Use these to guide you during the interview, or when it feels appropriate to use the Answer/Ask technique. Most interviewers will leave time at the end of the interview for you to ask questions, so be sure to take advantage of this opportunity. Asking good questions demonstrates your interest in the job and can give you an advantage over other candidates. For more information on the best questions to ask, check out the chapter titled 'Best Questions That Candidates Ask the Interviewer'.

Being unprofessional.

It's essential to maintain proper posture during the interview and avoid fidgeting with your hands or feet or any items around you. An interviewer once shared with me a story about a candidate who put their feet up on a chair during the interview, and another who was chewing gum. While these may seem like minor issues, they can create a negative impression. Keep in mind that during an interview, you are expected to be at your best, and anything less may lead the interviewer to wonder how you might behave as an employee. To avoid such mishaps, it's best to maintain a professional demeanor throughout the interview process.

Give a bad impression of your personality.

When interviewing for a job, be aware that certain personality traits may lead the interviewer to screen you out of the hiring process. Although interviewers do not explicitly test you for these traits, their experience in hiring informs them on how these traits can lead to problematic hires. These traits come up in discussions with hiring managers and impact the decision-making process. This is especially true for startups where smaller teams require employees to work closely with each other. While you cannot change your personality, it is important to be self-aware and avoid projecting these traits.

Top personality traits that interviewers watch out for.

1. Overly self-absorbed.
2. Dishonest/untrustworthy.
3. Inability to take responsibility for mistakes, especially by blaming others.
4. Inflexible and not open to new ideas, suggestions, or coaching. (I would include the "know-it-all" candidates in this category.)
5. Fragile ego that is unable to process constructive criticism.
6. Reckless risk taking. (Calculated risk taking is great, but careless actions are not.)
7. Bitter/angry or anything else that might indicate a future toxic co-worker/employee.

It's essential to treat every interaction with any company employee as a type of interview. Candidates might perform well in the interview with the hiring manager but fail to get the job because of a negative impression from the receptionist or anyone else they interact with. It's also important to keep up your professional demeanor in every meeting or conversation, even if it's a casual one. A moment of letting your guard down and saying something inappropriate can jeopardize your chances of getting hired. Always remember that every interaction is a chance to make a positive impression and be considered for the position.

How to Stand Out from Others

The employer's selection process is like a funnel, with numerous candidates entering at the top, and fewer progressing through each stage. As you move through the process, the company evaluates you and your competition, gathering feedback from everyone who interviews you. To be the candidate offered the job, you need to make a lasting impression from the very beginning.

Start by gaining a deep understanding of the position beyond what's in the job ad. Knowing what makes an ideal hire for the role will help you stand out. Reach out to your professional network for insights on the personality traits and skills that are successful in the position. Additionally, research the company, department, and interviewer to get a better sense of what they are looking for in a candidate.

During the interview, try to establish a personal connection with the interviewer. If you have any similarities with them, such as a shared background or interest, use that to your advantage. Be natural and relatable, and don't forget to use their name when speaking or sending an email. Take note of the names of those you meet and refer to them in the future.

Remember, your dream job is also someone else's dream. To stand out, you must do the small things that create a positive memory of your interactions with the company and its employees.

Here are a few things that will help you stand out.

Be fully prepared.
Before your interview, it is crucial to do your research on the company, its history, strategy, and executives. Take note of any information you can gather about the individuals who will be conducting your interviews. This pre-interview preparation will have a significant impact on the actual interview, and will help you establish a connection with the interviewer. The more you know about the company, the more comfortable you will feel answering their questions and the more insightful your questions

will be. Use this knowledge to your advantage during the interview and show the interviewer that you are invested in the company and the position.

Keep in mind that your interview will begin as soon as you arrive at the organization.

During job interviews, many companies request feedback from their front desk staff on the applicant's attitude. To present yourself as organized and professional, make sure you have the name of your interviewer and the time of your appointment. Practice polite and professional behavior, including your tone and body language. Remember that as soon as you step inside the building, you are in interview mode and should conduct yourself accordingly.

Unique Value Proposition (UVP).

Crafting a UVP is a powerful tool to establish your personal candidate brand during an interview. It is a concise version of your response to the "Tell me about yourself" question, highlighting your top skills and attributes that overlap with the ideal profile. Your statement should be no longer than thirty seconds, or three to four sentences. This statement can serve as an introduction at job fairs or networking events, or as a way to start a conversation during an interview. You can also use it to support your other answers by providing examples of your skills. For more guidance on crafting an effective UVP statement, refer to the companion workbook.

Be a good listener and answer the questions asked of you.

It may seem obvious, but many candidates start formulating their answer before the interviewer has finished asking the question. This can cause them to miss important details and leave out parts of their answer, giving the impression that they are not good listeners. If you don't listen carefully during the interview, the employer may assume that you will not follow directions or take feedback well on the job. Therefore, it is important to listen carefully to each question and make sure that you fully understand it before providing an answer.

Answer/Ask.

The majority of interviews are structured in a one-sided way where the interviewer asks the questions, and the candidate responds. However, the most impressive candidates are not only able to provide answers but also engage in a professional conversation with the interviewer. This Answer/Ask technique was previously mentioned in the chapter on The Dos and Don'ts of Interviewing. While it may require practice, it can be very effective when executed properly. It should not come across as forced or interrupt the interviewer, but rather should be a natural back-and-forth exchange. A follow-up question can be asked about thirty percent of the time after answering a question, which demonstrates confidence and engagement.

Example: If you are a business analyst and are asked about which ERP systems you have worked with at your last job, answer the question, and then ask something about their ERP system; which system do they use, which version, how long have they used it, how does the interviewer like it? Do not let the interview go too far off-course, but a natural back and forth will make you stand out in a positive way.

Forgive yourself if you make a mistake in the process.
Mistakes happen during interviews, but how you react to them can make all the difference. It's an opportunity to demonstrate resilience and composure in the face of adversity. It is essential to focus on the moment and not allow a mistake to ruin the rest of the meeting. Acknowledge the error, but quickly pivot back to the current question as if it were the first. Interviewers will remember how you handle the situation and your ability to recover more

than the mistake itself. This is a chance to show your ability to handle setbacks professionally and with confidence.

Pay attention to the little things.

Small things often make a big impact when it comes to building a positive impression of yourself as a job candidate. Arrive ten to fifteen minutes early for any in-person interview to demonstrate your punctuality and reliability. If you are going to be late, be sure to communicate with the recruiter or hiring manager in advance. Sending thank-you emails or notes after your interviews is also an important detail that many candidates overlook. While these may seem like simple gestures, they can make all the difference in setting you apart from other applicants who do not take the time to do them.

Closing statement.

When ending an interview, it is crucial to leave a lasting impression on the interviewer. Make sure to express gratitude for their time, convey that you enjoyed meeting them, show interest in the next steps of the process, and give a brief summary of what makes you a good fit for the role.

It's essential to be genuine and specific with your answers. Avoid using rehearsed or monotone responses, as this may cause you to fade into the background or be easily forgotten. Additionally, refrain from over-exaggerating your skills and abilities.

Ultimately, what sets a candidate apart is their unique characteristics and attributes that can benefit the manager and the company. By following the advice in this chapter, you can impress the interviewer and showcase the skills and traits that make you stand out from other candidates.

Best Questions That Candidates Ask the Interviewer

As you near the end of your interview, you will likely be asked if you have any questions for the interviewer. This is a crucial opportunity to gain insights into whether the job is a good fit for your goals, showcase your suitability for the position, and refine your understanding of the ideal profile. Failing to ask questions gives the impression that you are not a serious candidate or are simply seeking any job at the moment.

To make a positive impression, you should ask insightful questions of your interviewers. You can incorporate questions throughout the interview using the Answer/Ask technique mentioned earlier. When asked about remaining questions, ask two or three of the most relevant ones. I have listed some of the best questions from candidates that I have heard below. Before your interview, compile a list of the most relevant seven to ten questions you like. This way, you will still have two or three at the end that were left unanswered. You can even save questions on your phone or on a piece of paper and refer to them during the interview.

(Quick note that most companies will be the ones to bring up compensation. DO NOT ask about compensation at the beginning of an interview process, it shows that your priorities are wrong.)

I have broken down the best questions into four categories:

About the interviewer.

"What was your background before being hired here? How has that benefited you?"

"What do you love most about working here?"

"How would you describe your own management style?"

"What do you enjoy doing outside of work?"

"Is this the career path that you envisioned for yourself when you got your start?"

"What do you wish you knew back when you were in my shoes?"

"Why did you decide to work here?"

Company culture.

"How would you describe the company culture here?"

"What type of employee has been most successful here?"

"What about an employee that did not work out here, why didn't they succeed?"

"What are new employees most surprised by in their first few months here?"

"Why do employees love to work here?"

"What type of hires do not last long with your company?"

Interest in being successful with the company.

"What would you need me to focus on in the first month on the job?"

"What additional responsibilities can be gained over time in this role?"

"What has been the biggest challenge for this role?"

"What are the biggest company goals for the next few years, and how does this position affect those goals?"

"What have people who reported to you in the past done to be successful?"

"What would I need to accomplish in the first year in this job for you to view me as a successful hire?"

"What do you want this role to accomplish in the first 90 days?"

"How do you measure success for the person in this role?"

"What advice would you give to the person you hire in order for them to be successful in this role?"

"What have past employees done to become successful in this type of role here?"

"What are the biggest challenges that the company faces, and how can I help in this role?"

"Who is the company's biggest competitor, and what can I do in this role to help beat them?"

"What is the one trait that you have seen in people who have been very successful in this type of role?"

Due diligence.

"How would you explain this job in your own words?"

"What about my background made you choose me for the interview?"

"What does the interview process look like?"

"Why is the position available?"

"How long has this position been open?"

(If it has already been a couple of months or longer, here is a follow-up: *"What seems to be missing from candidates you have interviewed so far?"*)

"What is your timeframe for hiring someone for this position?"

"What do you think the company's biggest accomplishments will be in the next few years?"

Closing for the offer.

"What skills or experience do you wish I had to make myself a better fit for this position?"

"What are the next steps in the process?"

"What can I clarify about my background to show you that I am the best fit for the job?"

"When would you need me to start?"

(Subtle way to get them to picture hiring you)

"Is there anything in my skills or experience that you feel I am lacking compared to what you are looking for?"

When it comes to the interview process, it's essential to remember that the interviewers will discuss their impressions and recommendations about each candidate throughout and at the end of the process. The questions that you ask or don't ask can significantly impact their decision-making. So, it's crucial to take the time to get it right.

Never say that you have no questions when asked. Use the information gained from your conversation to make any necessary changes for your next interview. Remember to be aware of the time and respect any indications that the interview is coming to a close. Avoid asking questions if the interviewer is running late, as this may cause them to become impatient and leave a negative impression about you.

Employer Red Flags

Preparing for an interview can help you become a stronger and more confident candidate. But it's important to remember that the interview is not just about demonstrating why you're the best match for the job. You are also evaluating the company to see if it's a good fit for you.

One way to approach interviewing is to compare it to dating. Like people looking for a romantic partner, employers have an ideal profile of what they want in an employee. They are not trying to determine if you're a good or bad person, but if you're a good fit for what they need.

Just like in dating, a one-sided evaluation process isn't ideal. You have your own idea of what you're looking for in a job and it's important to pay attention to any red flags that may arise during the interview process. Don't be fooled by false positive impressions that could lead to a bad or toxic work situation.

By being aware of what you're looking for and paying attention to any warning signs, you can approach the interview process with more confidence and increase your chances of finding a good match for both you and the company.

Here are employer red flags for you to be extremely cautious of.

Asking you illegal interview questions.

The legality of questions that employers are allowed to ask varies by country and state. It is important to research and understand what can and cannot be asked where you and the employer are located. For example, in the United States, questions regarding age, religion, race, national origin, gender, marital status, pregnancy, or disability are not allowed. In some states, questions about current compensation are also prohibited. However, you can be asked if your age meets a legal requirement for the job, if you are authorized to work in the country, and if you can physically perform the job duties.

136

If you are asked a question that you believe is prohibited, it is not recommended to be confrontational. Try to answer the question without providing protected information. If the interviewer persists or there is a pattern of illegal questions, politely end the interview and leave. Most countries have a government agency to report such incidents if necessary. It is important to pay attention to red flags, as asking illegal questions can indicate what kind of employer they will be.

High employee turnover compared to other companies in the same industry.

While some employers may experience temporary high employee turnover due to changes in management or strategy, it is important to be cautious of those with a history of frequent turnover. Even if the opportunity seems promising on paper, take the time to understand the reasons behind their high turnover rate.

To gather more information, you can research the company on LinkedIn and compare the number of current employees to previous employees. Additionally, look at the length of time current employees have been with the company. If many employees have been there for less than a year, it could indicate rapid expansion or high turnover. It is crucial to thoroughly evaluate any potential employer to avoid finding yourself in a work environment with a history of instability and turnover.

The description of the job in the interview does not match the description in the ad / or is very unclear.

When an employer describes a different job or is unclear about what the position entails during the interview, it could be a classic bait-and-switch tactic. Employers use this tactic when they realize that the job isn't that attractive. If the job description they give you during the interview is different from what was advertised, it's essential to question a few things. If they change the job description once, will they do it again in the future? How bad is the job if they cannot provide a clear description of it?

Negative atmosphere.

Observing the behavior of employees in a company can give you a good idea of the work environment. Pay close attention to the interaction between co-workers, especially if you are on-site for an interview. Take note of how many employees seem to like each other and appear to be happy working together. If the employees, who are the ones that know the company's work culture best, do not seem content or satisfied, then you should consider that it could be you in the near future. So, be attentive to how the employees behave and interact, as it can be an important factor in deciding whether or not to pursue a job opportunity at the company.

Disrespectful of your time.

When interviewing for a job, it is common courtesy for both the interviewer and the interviewee to respect each other's time. However, there are times when a delay or an unforeseen event may cause the interviewer to be late. In such situations, the interviewer should be apologetic and respectful towards the candidate, who had to wait. This is a red flag that should not be ignored. If the interviewer does not respect your time during the interview process, it is unlikely that they will respect you once you become an employee. While there is no need to be impolite, this behavior should warn you about the kind of culture you may be working in if you accept the job.

Compensation does not match expectations.

When it comes to discussing compensation during the interview process, some companies will disclose the range at the beginning, while others will bring it up at the end. It is crucial to do your research beforehand and have a good understanding of the market value for your position, level of experience, and education. If a company appears to have champagne tastes on a beer budget, be cautious, as it may indicate a culture of expecting more from their employees than they are willing to pay for. However, there are exceptions, such as jobs where gaining experience is the greatest value or startups that may offer equity in the company as compensation. Remember to consider all aspects of the compensation package, including benefits and growth opportunities, when evaluating an offer.

They are asking you to complete free work as part of the interview process.

If a company asks you to complete unpaid work that is part of their regular business, it is a big red flag. Many interview processes include steps where you may be asked to complete a hypothetical exercise as an evaluation tool to test your skill level. However, asking candidates to do work for free is unacceptable, and it should be a warning sign. If their culture permits them to exploit job candidates, then how do you think they are going to treat you as an employee?

Negative company reviews.

Before you go in for an interview, make sure to research reviews online and within your professional network from former employees of the company. Keep in mind that disgruntled former employees may have a bias when writing those reviews, so use it more as a guide to things you should question rather than unimpeachable facts. Look for patterns where the same negative comments are made by multiple former employees. These patterns should be red flags, especially if they relate to your main concerns about the job or company.

During your interview process, pay attention to things you see or hear that match what the negative reviews claim. Take the opportunity to ask questions about any concerns you may have in a respectful and professional manner. This will not only help you to better understand the company's culture and practices, but it will also show the interviewer that you are proactive and engaged in the process.

You are asked about how you have dealt with working with difficult people.

If you hear variations of the question 'Can you deal with difficult people?' multiple times during your interview process, it might be a warning sign of a negative or toxic work environment. Although hearing this question once in an interview is not necessarily a red flag, it is still important to ask follow-up questions to gain a better understanding of the role and the people you may be working with. When answering this question, use the Answer/Ask technique to gather more information. If you get a negative answer, be aware that it could be a sign of difficult co-workers. Be cautious of phrases like 'they have high standards,' 'they're a perfectionist,' or 'they take some getting used to.' These statements could be a warning of a challenging work environment.

They gossip about previous employees.

A toxic workplace can cause a lot of problems, so it is important to avoid them. Gossip is one of the most toxic behaviors that can exist in a workplace, and if an interviewer engages in this behavior during an interview, it is a sign that the company has a toxic culture. If they are willing to smear a former employee's reputation to make themselves look better to you, they will likely do the same thing to you in the future. This is a huge red flag, and you should proceed with caution.

Like dating, the interview process is about finding a good match between employer and employee. Confident and likable people tend to do better in both. It is important to confidently present yourself as a good fit for the job, but also evaluate the employer to see if it is a good fit for you. Ignoring red flags during the evaluation stage can lead to regret later on. Keep presenting yourself as a good match, but continue to ask legitimate questions professionally during the interview process. A good employer will see this as a sign that you are serious about a long-term working relationship.

M. L. Miller

What to Expect from Different Interview Processes

Employers adopt diverse interview formats, and candidates may feel bewildered and distracted when they encounter a format that they did not anticipate. To assist you in navigating through these different interview types, I have compiled a list below, providing details on each one. This will help you become familiar with them, instill confidence, and allow you to remain focused on your objective should you ever encounter them.

Interview formats.

1-on-1.
The one-on-one interview is the most familiar type for job seekers. During this interview, you and the interviewer will have a discussion about your background and the opportunity. The

majority of the advice in this book can be directly applied to this type of interview.

1-on-1 sequential.

A series of one-on-one interviews constitutes the sequential interviewing process, where you progress to the next round of interviews if you perform well. Most people are familiar with this format, but it is worth noting that these processes usually culminate in a final interview, which may use one of the other interview formats.

Panel.

The panel interview can be an intimidating experience for candidates. This type of interview involves one candidate meeting with two or more interviewers at the same time. Typically, there are between three to five interviewers on a panel. Employers conduct panel interviews to expedite the hiring process, make collaborative hiring decisions based on seeing and hearing the same things, and train new interviewers. To succeed in a panel interview, it is crucial to remain calm and confident, and avoid focusing solely on one interviewer. Instead, make good eye contact with everyone on the panel, spending slightly more time with the interviewer who asked the question. After the interview, all the interviewers will provide feedback on your suitability for the role, so it is essential to create as many advocates on the panel as possible.

Half/full day.

The half/full day of interviewing format is typically reserved for the final stage of an interview process, as it allows multiple stakeholders to participate in the hiring decision. During this type of interview, you will typically meet with your potential manager, peers, human resources representatives, managers from other teams or departments, and the hiring manager's boss. It is essential to maintain your energy and enthusiasm throughout the day, as this format can be long and arduous. Pay attention to staying hydrated and eating or snacking as needed. It is worth noting that I once had a great candidate perform exceptionally well in the morning interviews, only to perform poorly in the afternoon due to a lack of energy. As a result, they were not hired. Therefore, be mindful of your energy level and enthusiasm in each interview to maximize your chances of success.

Informal.

An informal interview is often used for senior positions, such as taking a candidate to lunch or dinner. However, it can also be as simple as having a peer give you a tour of the facility or chatting with you in the lobby. One common mistake that candidates make during informal interviews is letting their guard down and forgetting that they are still being evaluated. It is crucial to remain relaxed yet professional, positive, and focused on demonstrating how you fit the ideal profile for the position. So, while you should strive to be as comfortable as possible during informal interviews, remember that it is still a part of the interview process.

Phone.

While an initial phone screen is typically a part of most interview processes, it can be included at any point along the way. One of the great advantages of conducting an interview over the phone is that the interviewer cannot see you, which allows you to have your notes, resume, job description, and profile in front of you during the interview. It may seem insignificant, but standing and smiling when you speak on the phone can create a more positive impression. Smiling will make your voice project more confidently and warmly. After the call (or video call) ends, take a few moments to jot down notes while the conversation is still fresh in your memory. Record any comments the interviewer made that provide more insight into the job duties, company culture, or any other information that can give you an advantage in future interviews.

Video.

Video interviews are becoming increasingly common and have presented a learning curve for some candidates. These interviews take place over video conferencing platforms such as Zoom, MS Teams, Google Meet, Skype, or similar platforms. I have seen some candidates turn off their cameras and only use audio during the interview. It is crucial to treat a video interview like an in-person meeting by dressing professionally and always keeping your camera turned on unless you have a technical issue. Many video conferencing platforms offer virtual backgrounds, which can be used if your physical background is distracting. I have also experienced interviews where the candidate's camera was placed to the side of their computer screen, making it appear as though they were not making eye contact. Before any video interview, make sure to test your camera and audio, and position the camera in a way that allows you to give the impression of making eye contact with the interviewer.

One-way video application.

Some companies have begun using pre-recorded video answers
to screening questions as part of the application process. In
addition to the advice that I gave for video interviews, you should
uncover the details of the settings for your video application.
Some will allow you to record a video as many times as you want
before submitting, while others will have a limit. With formats
that limit the times that you can record, you can practice your
answers using your smartphone before recording in the
application itself.

Peer.

Interviews conducted by potential future co-workers can occur in
a formal 1-on-1, panel, video, or casual setting. Such interviews
provide a unique perspective and offer insights that may not be
available through other interview formats. However, these
interviews are also riddled with potential pitfalls. Some
candidates may feel overly relaxed when speaking with a peer,
which may result in giving negative responses or asking
inappropriate questions that they would not ask the hiring
manager. To succeed in your interview process, it is essential to
remember that you are always being interviewed, and the peer
will likely be asked about their interaction with you. So, always

maintain a professional demeanor, regardless of who you are speaking to during the interview process.

Stress.

If you are interviewing for a job that will require you to deal with stressful situations, then it is a good idea for the employer to find out how you handle yourself under stress. When I have used this technique, I typically change my tone of voice and act more aggressively towards the candidate, but stress interviews can take on different forms. At the very least you should expect to be asked uncomfortable or stressful questions that are meant to emulate the type of stress in this job. The most successful way to prepare for this type of interview is to do enough research to know whether to expect one. Being surprised by these types of interviews increases the chances of failure. If you do recognize that you are being tested on how you handle stress, try to think about the ideal profile they are trying to hire and do what you can to demonstrate how you would respond if hired. When you are researching the company, do a search with the company name and "Stress Interview" to see if this is something you should expect.

Group.

Group interviews involve a group of candidates meeting with one or a few interviewers at once. While I am not a big fan of this type of interview, its primary purpose is to quickly eliminate candidates. The interviewer will gather several candidates and give a presentation about the job opportunity, which may not be the most attractive job available on the market. Candidates not interested in the position will be instructed to leave, and the interviewer will continue with the remaining candidates. There is not much advice I can offer to perform well in this type of interview as it is more about determining whether the job aligns with your interests. However, ensure that you ask questions and comprehend the role. The reason many employers use a group interview format is that numerous candidates have previously declined the job offer. As such, you should question why this is the case and decide accordingly.

The Job Offer

After successfully completing the interview process, you may have an offer of employment coming your way. Although companies typically make verbal offers, most will follow up with a written offer letter. Your offer will likely have an expiration date since employers need to move on to the next candidate if you decline the offer. One week is the standard time frame, and while you can negotiate the deadline, asking for two or more weeks may suggest that the offer is not your top choice.

While most candidates do not negotiate job offers, those who do tend to earn more money. Negotiating the details of a job offer is more successful if you have followed the advice in this book and created a high-value candidate image with the company. The most crucial piece of advice is that you should negotiate your job offer in most cases. Conduct research to increase your chances of success.

Salary is not the only aspect you can negotiate. Depending on the company, you can request better shifts, company equity, education or training reimbursement, more responsibilities to gain experience, and other benefits.

For more information on successful salary negotiation, please read *SoaringME.com Guide to Successful Salary Negotiation*. However, be cautious when seeking other advice, as I have seen poor advice given by unqualified individuals.

When asked about your salary expectations, avoid staying silent as some suggest. Playing negotiation games may work in some limited cases, but it is not always effective. If an employer wants to hire you, they may overlook any concerns they have about your behavior. However, most of the time, playing negotiation games may make you appear untrustworthy or misguided. Instead, prepare to answer the question about your salary expectations professionally and know what a fair and realistic market price is for your services.

If you found this book to be valuable, please remember to leave a rating to let others know.

Visit SoaringME.com or ask your favorite bookstore for our other books to help your career.

About the Author

M.L. Miller was born in Washington state, grew up in Oregon and, having lived in various places around the United States, he is now back living in the Pacific Northwest with his wife, Wilawan.

Having studied Economics/Finance at the University of Hartford in Connecticut, M.L. began a career in recruitment in 1997, working for hundreds of client companies from Fortune 100 large companies to start-ups. During this time, he has conducted somewhere between twenty and thirty thousand job interviews and has hired thousands of employees in a variety of roles from entry-level positions to C-Suite and Board-Level. During his career he managed a corporate recruiting team, increasing their hires by over 33% in under two years. He started Ethical Recruiters, Inc., an executive recruitment firm and later SoaringME, a company that educates candidates on how to be more successful in job interviewing.

Within this framework, M.L. has also published several books related to the subject:

·   *SoaringME The Ultimate Guide to Successful Job Searching.*

·   *SoaringME The Ultimate Guide to Successful Job Interviewing.*

·   *SoaringME COMPANION WORKBOOK The Ultimate Guide to Successful Job Interviewing.*

·   *SoaringME.com: Guide to Successful Salary Negotiation.*

He also has several Ultimate Guides on interviewing for specific careers.

In his free time, M.L. is an avid cyclist and has ridden the annual 200-mile Seattle-to-Portland bike ride five times so far. He also enjoys traveling domestically and internationally.

M.L. has worked with homeless military veterans for a couple of years through a non-profit organization. He used his experience to help them improve interviewing skills, write resumes, and obtain employment to get back on their feet. He also raises money for children's mental health charities.

In the future, M.L. plans to continue his career in talent acquisition. His personal goal is to one day combine his love of cycling and travel to complete 100-mile bike rides on five different continents.

His favorite quote is "Every strike brings me closer to the next home run..." – Babe Ruth.

www.ingramcontent.com/pod-product-compliance
Lightning Source LLC
Chambersburg PA
CBHW060932220326
41597CB00020BA/3527